DIESEL-HYDRAULIC LOCOMOTIVES

OF THE WESTERN REGION

David & Charles Locomotive Studies

Locomotive Monographs

General Editor:

O. S. Nock, BSc, CEng, FICE, FIMechE

DAVID & CHARLES LOCOMOTIVE STUDIES

DIESEL-HYDRAULIC
LOCOMOTIVES
OF THE
WESTERN REGION

BRIAN REED

DAVID & CHARLES

NEWTON ABBOT   LONDON

NORTH POMFRET (VT)   VANCOUVER

ISBN 0 7153 6769 2

First published 1975
Second impression 1978

All rights reserved. No part of this publication
may be reproduced, stored in a retrieval system
or transmitted in any form or by any means
electronic, mechanical, photocopying, recording
or otherwise without the prior permission of
David & Charles (Publishers) Limited

Printed in Great Britain
by Redwood Burn Ltd.,
Trowbridge & Esher
for David & Charles (Publishers) Limited
Brunel House Newton Abbot Devon

Published in the United States of America by
David & Charles Inc North Pomfret Vermont
05053 USA

Published in Canada
by Douglas David & Charles Limited
1875 Welch Street North Vancouver BC

CONTENTS

Diesel-Hydraulic C-C D1035 Western Yeoman *pulls
out of Bristol Temple Meads on a 10-coach
express for Penzance*

G. F. Heiron

CHAPTER 1

THE MODERNISATION PLAN

ALONE among the five Regions of British Railways (BR) the Western Region (WR) concentrated on hydraulic transmission for line-service diesel locomotives ordered under the Modernisation Plan introduced in 1955. At a time when other Regions fell into line with a headquarters policy of nearly a dozen diesel-electric locomotive types of 800 to 2300bhp, the WR stood firm for two types with turbo transmissions, and visualised no more than three or four locomotive models being required exclusive of shunting duties. All these classes were to have quick-running engines; classes on other Regions were to have slow-running engines entirely, or certainly a large proportion of them, plus a few quick-running types allied to electric transmission.

Through 1954, under a remit from the Government, an internal committee of higher British Transport Commission (BTC) and BR personnel studied the provision of 'equipment, in the widest sense of that word, of modern design and fit to give reliable and speedy transport service on a large scale'. A report submitted to the Minister of Transport in January 1955 envisaged a 15-year plan with an outlay around £1200 million to cover continuous brakes on nearly all freight wagons, diesel traction, electrification, remodelled freight services including modern marshalling yards, and up-to-date signalling and telecommunications. In effect this was given approval within two months by the second reading of the Transport (Borrowing Powers) Bill.

Estimated expenditure of about £125 million in the 15 years was submitted for 2500 line-service diesel locomotives, plus £25 million for about 1200 shunting and freight transfer locomotives to replace 1500 steam shunters. The proposals envisaged comparatively few high power locomotives, because prices at the time averaged £50 to £55/bhp, which meant an average of only 900/1000bhp for the 2500 units. A further large sum was allotted to 4600 diesel railcars and trailers, including 300 vehicles already on order. At that time BR possessed 18,800 steam locomotives plus 400 diesel and straight electric locomotives, equal to approximately one locomotive for every route mile of line. Few railways in the world had such a density of motive power.

Though no new steam locomotives were to be sanctioned after the 1956 construction programme £10 million was allotted in the plan for steam depot modernisation.

No high power diesel locomotives had been put in hand by the nationalised BR since its formation on 1 January 1948, and the stock in 1955 comprised the LM Region Nos 10000 and 10001 of 1600bhp, the three SR units Nos 10201–3 of 1750/2000bhp, and the Fell diesel-mechanical locomotive of 2000bhp, most of which had been completed under BR though initiated by Group companies. The Fell locomotive was not entirely the property of BR at that time, though later it became so. There was also one 800bhp diesel-electric locomotive No 10800.

A principle of 'pilot orders' for about 170 diesel locomotives of 800 to 2000bhp was sanctioned in May 1955. In the following November details were announced of orders for 171 locomotives of no fewer than 13 different types; in January 1956 they were supplemented, at the instance of the WR, by a further order for three locomotives of yet another design. Of the 14 orders aggregating 174 locomotives and costing over £10 million, three, representing 14 units, were for diesel-hydraulic locomotives to WR requirements. Of the total, 141 locomotives were to be supplied by private manufacturers and 33 by BR workshops; the power-transmission control equipments for the latter were to come from outside contractors.

The great spread of pilot orders was to allow comparative trials to determine which were likely to be the best types in the different power classifications, for until that time no constructive thought had been given to main line diesel traction by the BR departments vitally concerned, which since 1948 had worked much on the concept of 'Steam in our time, O Lord. Amen.' Despite this, the 'expert advice as to the capacity of the available technical staff' on electrification taken by the BTC was not extended to diesel traction. That was unfortunate, for all the work in getting, testing and choosing from innumerable designs was for a motive power system regarded in the modernisation plan, for main lines at least, as only a temporary solution preceding full electrification.

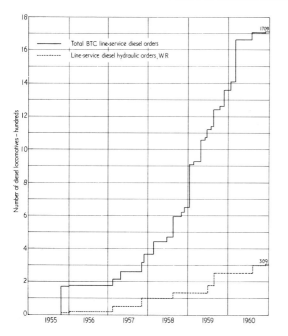

Fig 1 *Build-up of BTC line-service diesel locomotive orders, 1955–61*

Seven years after the pilot orders were announced there was still no sign of that standardisation which the modernisation report had stressed as essential, and which the first chairman of the BTC, Sir Brian Robertson, had felt was one of the prime aims. On the contrary, the urgency for modernisation and the lengthy periods before delivery of most of the 174 pilot locomotives were such that further large orders had to be placed when only one of the 14 pilot types had begun to appear; before the summer of 1961 there were in service or on order 1781 line-service diesel locomotives of 22 different classes with another half dozen variations, and grouped in 55 separate orders.

Of these, 309 were WR diesel-hydraulics in

five classes, one of which was in two variations. The five groups were known on the WR as the D600, D6300, D800, D1000 and D7000 (Hymek) classes, and made up the whole of the WR acquisition. At no time did WR diesel-hydraulics represent more than 18 per cent of BR line-service diesel locomotive stock, and for most of the time the proportion was not above 14 per cent. Build up of these BTC and WR orders is shown in Fig 1.

In 1964 BR itself introduced a 650bhp freight transfer six-wheeler with hydraulic drive of which 56 were built at Swindon for Western and Eastern Regions. Known as the 9500 class, and from the end of 1968 as class 14, they were the shortest-lived of all BR diesels and were scrapped or sold out of service in 1969–70, some after a working life of only three years. They were not part of the basic WR diesel-hydraulic concept, and are thus not considered here.

Originally the line-service diesel locomotives of BR were to be grouped in three power classifications, denoted by A for units of 750 to 1000bhp, B for units above 1000bhp and up to 1999bhp, and C for units of 2000bhp upwards. In May 1957, as the first of the pilot-order locomotives were coming into traffic, a numbering system with the prefix D was introduced for the forthcoming diesels, in which blocks of numbers were to be allocated to different outputs, so that at one glance a locomotive could be identified and some indication gained of its power. However, in November the same year power-group letters were abandoned in favour of a digit system in which the lowest number represented the lowest power range. These power type numbers, 1 to 5, were used from the time of the actual deliveries, and are shown alongside the previous scheme in Table I. The only type to come within class 5 was the Deltic.

In the autumn of 1968 yet another numerical classification system was introduced on BR, with class numbers in the range 1 to 55 for diesel locomotives and from 70 to 86 for straight electric locomotives. On the WR the D6300 class became class 22, the Hymeks class 35, and the D1000s class 52. The D800 was divided into class 42 for Maybach-engined units and class 43 for MAN-powered locomotives. By

Table I—BR Original diesel numbering and classification

Duty	Original power class	Final power class	Original number blocks	Renumbering scheme 11/1957	Original hp range
Line-service	C	4	1-2499	D1-999	2000/2500
Line-service	C	5	—	D1000-1999	3000
Shunting	—	—	2500-2999	D2000-2999	150/300
Shunting	—	—	3000-4999	D3000-4999	350
Line-service	B	2	5000-7999	D5000-6499	1000/1250
Line-service	B	3	—	D6500-7999	1500/1750
Line-service	A	1	8000-8999	D8000-8999	750/1000
Miscellaneous	—	—	—	D9000-9999	—

The Western Region's first diesel-hydraulic locomotive, D600, on trial in Scotland, December 1957, before delivery to Swindon

this time the five locomotives of class D600 had been withdrawn, so no new classification was needed. Throughout this book the WR class numbers are used, having been borne by the locomotives for the greater part of their lives.

Towards the end of 1968 when the last standard gauge steam locomotives were withdrawn, use of the prefix D was given up. On WR locomotives with cast number plates the D at first was simply painted black or the body colour that happened to be on at the time. Concurrently, information panels were added to the cab sides, giving class number, weight, braking force, route availability, and maximum permitted speed. Yet another BR renumbering scheme was introduced in 1973; but as the surviving WR diesel-hydraulics (then only Hymeks and D1000s) were scheduled for withdrawal in 1974 no numbers under the new scheme were allotted to them.

The Whyte system of wheel notation used almost universally for steam locomotives since around 1900 cannot readily be applied to diesel locomotives, which are described instead by a modification of the old European method of denoting steam locomotive axle arrangements by letters of the alphabet for the number of driving and coupled axles, and figures for carrying axles. Here A represents a single driving axle, B two driving axles, C three driving axles and so on, an Atlantic being 2B1 and a Pacific 2C1.

In diesel locomotives the letters B, C, D and E in themselves give no indication as to how the axles are driven or connected; therefore a small cypher, or o, is added as a suffix behind the main letter when the axles have motors or drives of their own, but not in the case of A, which cannot be anything else but individually driven. An ordinary double-bogie diesel locomotive with two axles in each bogie is a Bo-Bo if it has a separate motor or drive for each axle, or a B-B if it has only one motor or master drive connected to each axle through rods, interconnected gears or shafts. A double-bogie locomotive with two three-axle bogies is Co-Co or C-C; sometimes only the two outer axles of such a bogie are driven, which gives an axle notation of A1A-A1A.

When a single pair of guiding wheels is attached to the outer end of each main power bogie a figure is added, for example 1–Co–Co–1 with pony trucks, or 2–Co–Co–2 with a four-wheel bogie at each end. If the guiding axles are not in trucks, but are carried within the main bogie underframe, then the notations are 1Co–Co1 and 2Co–Co2. Other variations to denote the location of drawgear and articulation of the two trucks had no application on BR.

A feature of diesel-hydraulics is that the driven axles in a bogie are almost always connected, the equivalent of 'coupled' in steam locomotives, whereas in diesel-electrics each driven axle

Table II—Western Region diesel-hydraulic classes

Wheel arrangement	Class Name	WR class No	BR 1968 class No	Loco bhp	No of locos built
A1A-A1A	Warship	D600	—	2000	5
B-B	—	D6300	22	1000/1100	58
B-B	Warship	D800	42 & 43	2070/2270	71
B-B	Hymek	D7000	35	1700	101
C-C	Western	D1000	52	2700	74

usually has a nose-suspended motor of its own, and without connection between the axles, so that an axle can slip on its own.

Of the 309 diesel-hydraulics built to BTC orders for the WR, 230 were B–B, 74 were C–C, and 5 were A1A–A1A, with a power range from 1000 to 2760bhp. They were confined to power classes 2, 3 and 4 (see Table I), and were grouped in the five main WR classes shown also in Table II. The first was delivered in December 1957 and the last in July 1964. The first withdrawals were in December 1967; the last locomotive was scheduled to be withdrawn by the end of 1974 to enable the whole of the BR diesel locomotive stock to be standardised on electric transmission and, with the exception of the Deltics, to be based on heavy slow-speed oil engines. The last main repair of a diesel-hydraulic at Swindon was completed in September 1973. Chronic shortage of motive power on the WR may however prolong the life of some D1000s into 1975.

CHAPTER 2

WHY DIESEL-HYDRAULICS FOR THE WESTERN?

PRIMARILY the adoption and adaptation of main line diesel locomotives by BR was to bring into effect the relevant terms of the modernisation plan (speed-up, punctuality, economy, efficiency) while dovetailing with such other measures as continuous brakes for freight stock. Types or makes of diesel locomotives, oil engines and transmissions were not prime factors in preliminary studies of diesel traction made to determine the necessary basic characteristics to be integrated with the whole railway operation. All the principles were considered by the WR, but investigations on that region proceeded from premises different from those adopted at BTC headquarters and in other regions, where there was an immediate predilection for heavy diesel-electrics as such, without examination of traction fundamentals or of the railway economics involved.

In the first place, higher management on the WR took the lead in the investigation of diesel traction, and then of diesel locomotive characteristics and types. They did not follow the conventional practice of leaving the regional mechanical engineer to make what enquiries he liked in conjunction with BTC mechanical headquarters, and then put up specific proposals for financial sanction. As the whole operation of the region was to be reborn, motive power had to be integrated completely with all other aspects, and was too important to be settled on a departmental or purely engineering basis.

Having studied the implications of the modernisation plan, and having taken part in the discussions preceding the issue of the report, chief officers of the WR appreciated that the fitting of automatic continuous brakes to the great majority of wagons was the greatest single measure towards the rejuvenation of national railway operation. It alone would enable all the slow trains to be speeded up, and would reduce considerably the speed gap between the fastest and the slowest trains. Freight train speed-up was also looked upon as an important factor contributing to increased utilisation of locomotives, which was essential to the economic success of the diesel part of the programme.

Any new motive power had to accord absolutely with the resulting speed-up of all goods trains as well as with the proposed acceleration of passenger trains. Thus high power:weight ratios would be necessary, particularly to provide higher rates of acceleration right up to the top permissible speed for any train, and to maintain a good steady speed up long inclines. High power:weight ratio also was a direct aid to punctuality as it enabled a train to be brought back to its right path at the earliest possible moment after an out-of-course delay.

On the other side of the scale, no longer would locomotives on any principle have to be made heavier than necessary for traction merely to provide greater braking weight for loose-coupled unbraked mineral and freight trains of up to 1000 tons and more trailing loads. For goods working adhesion weight need be no more than that set by the required starting tractive effort under the most onerous combination of grade, load and rail condition, or by the strength of the couplings adopted, whichever was the smaller.

Checks showed that a starting effort around 42,000/44,000lb would be sufficient to meet WR maximum requirements whether freight trains were braked or not. It would also be up to the maximum that could be taken by three-link couplings, and close to the desirable limit for standard screw couplings if those were applied to all braked freight stock in place of loose couplings. There was no difficulty at all in exceeding 40,000lb maximum effort with diesel locomotives of 1000hp and upwards. The problem was to keep the starting efforts below useless peaks that would merely break couplings.

With the even torque throughout a wheel revolution provided by acceptable transmission systems, and the gradual application of power through a multi-notch control, a factor of adhesion above 3.8 was unnecessary. This meant an adhesion weight of about 72 tons with fuel

Left upper: *B-B 2270bhp Warship No D311 of the second Swindon batch in Ranelagh Bridge sidings, Royal Oak, before taking over a down express from Paddington, July 1960*
British Railways

Left lower: *BR 1Co-Co1 diesel-electric of 138 tons weight and equivalent in engine hp to the 78½ ton B-B Warship diesel-hydraulics of the WR*
British Railways

D1041 Western Prince *at the head of the Royal*
train passing Hawkeridge Junction on June 3, 1966
Ivo Peters

tanks and any train-heating water tanks three-
quarters empty, or no more than 80 tons with
all supplies on board. In practice the torque-
multiplying features of both hydraulic and electric transmissions provide starting efforts so high
that factors of adhesion are more often just taken
as 3.33, or 30 per cent adhesion.

At this stage in WR investigations BTC technical headquarters favoured type 4 diesel-electric
proposals involving well over 100 tons of adhesion
weight. Moreover, those designs had additional
carrying axles supporting still more weight so
that estimated locomotive totals were 125 tons
and over. Viewed from the aspects of railway
mechanics and economical railway operation such
ideas did not make sense to WR higher management, particularly when an overall opportunity
had come to get new equipment that was not an
extension of the old, and had no limitations set
by the old except loading gauge, axle load,
linear loading, and buffer-coupling height.

Was there any possibility in type 4 diesels of
getting much closer to the optimum adhesion
weight in conjunction with an engine output that
would give performance on the line equal to that
of a King class four-cylinder 4–6–0 steam loco-

motive, but with more rapid acceleration from
rest and from service slacks, in conjunction with
a lower axle load? The answer seemed to be
'yes' after the WR realised that in 1953–54 the
German Federal Railway (Deutsche Bundesbahn,
or DB) had introduced five 80-ton B–B 2000bhp
diesel-hydraulic locomotives that by the summer
of 1955 were averaging 10,000 miles/month/loco
in daily express train haulage.

Immediate appreciation that the 80 tons of
adhesion weight also represented the total weight
of locomotives running smoothly each day up to
70/75mph led WR top management to crystallise
its objections to the numerous heavy diesel-electric
propositions then being formulated by the BTC
technical authorities as: (*a*) a 125/135-ton locomotive seemed unreasonable if one of 80 tons was
possible for the same engine power, traffic performance and axle load; (*b*) presumably some
additional cost would be involved in the extra 45
to 50 tons of material even if that material and
the equipment were not so refined as in the lighter
locomotive; (*c*) the extra ineffective weight would
have to be dragged about throughout the life of
the locomotive at the cost of increased fuel consumption, which at the levels expected from the

modernisation plan, and with fuel at its then cost of 14d/gal, could amount to £18,000 to £20,000 a year on the basis of 100 locomotives; (d) an 80-ton diesel-hydraulic might well have a haulage capacity of one, or even two, coaches more than a 130-ton diesel-electric on exacting passenger schedules; (e) presumably four axles, eight axleboxes and four drives would occupy less time daily and periodically in preparation and maintenance, and would consume less lubricant, than the eight axles, 16 axleboxes and six gear-drive traction motors of the 1Co–Co1 diesel-electrics; and (f) the conception behind those huge diesel-electrics seemed in opposition to the whole object of the modernisation plan.

Further, the WR operated no electrified mileage, and had no conversion scheme in sight. There was no desire to set up a heavy-electrical repair and maintenance organisation; feeling was that personnel then engaged in steam locomotive repairs could be trained more easily and effectively to deal with hydraulic transmissions and the associated gears than to do electrical work.

Another advantage was that for any given power and adhesion weight the continuous rated tractive effort from hydraulic transmission could be substantially higher, and at a lower speed, than was economically practicable with electric transmission, and without any diminution in permissible top speed. This would be an important factor on the WR, for it meant that one and the same locomotive would be equally effective over the 1 in 37 to 1 in 80 grades between Newton Abbot and Penzance and on the preceding 190-mile high speed stretch between London and Newton Abbot. Finally, the vague pilot-order scheme taking shape meant that diesel-hydraulics were in no way impeding the modernisation plan as seen by its implementers, but were providing a promising further alternative for unbiased appraisal.

In no way did the WR draw towards diesel-hydraulics because fluid drive was considered a better transmission, as such, than electric. True, it had a lower weight; but as far as mechanical efficiency, utilisation of full engine power, and near stepless control went there was never anything to choose between the two. In general, diesel-hydraulic line-service locomotives had quick running lightweight oil engines, though there was no engineering reason barring the coupling up of low speed types. The WR decision was taken because hydraulic drive in conjunction with the principles of locomotive design already adopted with success elsewhere seemed to offer

a far better power:weight ratio, lower locomotive weight, higher drawbar efficiency, a more compact design, greater ability to cope with steep grades and high top speeds, and a possibility of smoother change-over of workshop facilities from steam, than any diesel-electric proposition then being bruited, and at a capital cost no greater than that of diesel-electrics.

Twin-engine installations did not seem to the management to be any great disadvantage, for though the number of moving parts would be more they would be lighter and more easily handled, and would require smaller lifting tackle and lower roof heights than would slow-speed engines of 2000bhp and more; they seemed more in accord with the then general engineering tendencies of small, light and easily handled interchangeable components. Brief enquiries had shown two such engines plus hydraulic transmissions, drives, and a complete control system would cost rather less than one big slow-speed engine plus electric transmission and control equipment.

At this stage the regional cme was instructed to confer with the BTC mechanical engineering department, and in conjunction with it to get definite proposals and prices for a few double-engine type 4 locomotives of around 2000bhp, plus a handful of single-engine type 2 units of half the output, and with engine, transmission and auxiliaries the same in each case. This matter did not prove so simple, as is related in chapter 4.

Until this time the moving spirit behind WR traction ideas had been H. H. Phillips, assistant general manager of the WR, who saw that the modernisation plan was likely to be the last opportunity for recasting the operation of the British railway system on a major scale; and as far as the WR was concerned he strove for this to be done on fundamentally correct principles that would also permit an easy transition in years to come to any further developments or newer techniques that might be evolved.

Phillips had been a Great Western or WR man all his professional life. His leading characteristic was that, though primarily an operator and administrator, and not a trained engineer, he had an instinctive grasp of railway mechanics, railway layout and operation. For the implementation of the modernisation plan he saw the over-riding importance of the brake question and of high power:weight ratios in motive power and trains; he felt there was no basic reason why diesel-hydraulic locomotives with quick-running oil engines should be inferior to diesel-electrics with slow-running engines in reliability and cost of maintenance and repair.

The cogent reasoning of Phillips received the backing of the regional general manager, K. W. C. Grand, and the regional chairman, R. F. Hanks, for WR concentration on diesel-hydraulics in the pilot scheme. Grand was an administrator who for many years had been closely associated with the central management at Paddington. Since nationalisation on 1 January 1948 he had been the WR chief regional officer, succeeding Sir James Milne, the last general manager of the Great Western Railway. Intuitively he viewed the WR as a whole, geographically and administratively, and wanted any new motive power to fit within full regional requirements on a standard basis and not with exceptions or limitations.

Hanks had left railway service in 1922 after training at Swindon works, and eventually succeeded Sir Miles Thomas as No 1 at Cowley in the Nuffield organisation. He came back to the WR as part-time chairman in 1955. To him, the lightweight quick-running internal-combustion engine and non-electric transmission were normal, as were high power: weight ratios, and he realised such factors were the common need, though in different degrees, of all forms of power transport.

The insistence and enthusiasm of these three men gradually gained the wholehearted support of the then regional cme, R. A. Smeddle, though in implementing technically the managerial decision, his path, of necessity linked to that of BTC mechanical engineering headquarters, was anything but smooth, for the latter department was perpetuating its limited and undigested experience with the five heavy diesel-electrics 10000–1 and 10201–3. The resulting commitment to diesel-electrics weighing 130 to 140lb/

bhp was a policy that took no account either of the forward-looking modernisation plan nor of the tremendous war-time advances in internal-combustion engine and transmission techniques, or of the large number of men who had become familiar with them in high-powered armoured fighting vehicles and ships.

Thus two completely different, and largely opposed, psychologies were at work on the motive power of the British railway system from 1955. They did not come to a settlement through the pilot orders, and indeed did not do so until the withdrawal of the last diesel-hydraulics in 1974–75.

However successful diesel-hydraulic traction might be, it could not be applied to all line-service diesel power on BR because there was not a British industry big enough to fulfil needs of that magnitude. But BR was supposed to be initiating a major change; as the national, but not nationalised, electrical industry showed only one small sign of making any real advance on Nos 10000–1, and the BTC central mechanical engineering department did not insist on modern techniques, there was reason for one region, at least, to make efforts to have motive power integrated with the stated new requirements.

Consideration of WR activities in diesel traction over the years 1955–62 needs constant reference back to the terms of the modernisation plan. The situation was inherently frictional, for the diesel-hydraulic locomotives favoured, and the types of machinery installed, resulted from WR efforts to implement that plan clearly and effectively. On the other hand, those locomotives were not WR but BTC property, and sanction for any order needed the prior formal approval of the BTC cme whose own preference was for something much different.

CHAPTER 3

WHAT ARE DIESEL-HYDRAULICS?

BEING unable to start itself, and being nearly a constant speed machine as far as economical and effective output is concerned, the diesel engine needs a starting mechanism, and then a transmission system to convert the power into variable speed and torque combinations at the wheels to give the constantly changing track speed and tractive effort required in train haulage. The control system to effect these variations is as important as the two main constituents.

With electric transmission the engine drives a main generator which furnishes current to the traction motors through the medium of control that brings the various combinations of amps and volts needed for tractive effort and speed. In the hydraulic principle the engine drives oil-filled turbo converters, the drive from which is through a combination of gears and cardan shafts. This system is known as hydrokinetic drive. There are also hydrostatic forms; but apart from the von Rolls-Badoni system up to 500hp they have not been applied to traction in post-second world war years.

In electric transmission, the producing, converting and utilising equipments are separate, and the final drive from the utiliser (the traction motors) to the axle is through simple single-reduction straight-tooth gears. In hydraulic drives the generating-converting-utilising components are in a single casing, but that casing may contain three sets of such elements, that is, three separate fluid circuits, only one of which is in use at a time. The final drive is through an aggregation of gears, cardans and spiral bevels.

All hydraulic turbo systems, and prominently the Voith and Mekydro types used by the WR, stem from the pre-1914 inventions of the German engineer Hermann Föttinger. Essences of the Voith system are that two or three fluid circuits are used in succession to cover the track speed range from zero to top, and that the change from one to the other is made by the emptying of the circuit in use coincident with the filling of the one to be brought into use. This emptying and filling is done automatically according to the track speed, which brings into circuit whichever converter or fluid coupling is best suited to the conditions. Because of the concurrent emptying and filling there is little drop in tractive effort

during the change, and what there is is of brief duration. Though both are of turbo form, fluid flywheels or couplings are essentially different from torque converters, being simply clutches in which the slip is taken up hydraulically instead of by friction discs. Though some Voith drives included fluid couplings, all on the WR were made up of three converters acting in series.

Also derived from Föttinger's early work, Maybach's Mekydro system has an important variation in principle in that only a single fluid circuit is used in a permanently-filled converter. Maybach supplied complete transmissions, and even designed and made cardan shafts. Basis of Mekydro is that the track speed range is covered by a change-speed gearbox behind the converter, usually with four steps covered by three pairs of wheels. The control gives automatic change whenever conditions of track speed necessitate. At each change the converter, though kept full, is momentarily disengaged axially. The practical operation is due much to the Maybach over-running claw clutch with automatic change, invented in the 1920s for automobiles, and much developed during World War II up to 1000hp. With this system, distinct from Voith, there is a complete break in tractive effort at each gear change, though as a rule this is only of a fraction of a second's duration.

Both Voith and Mekydro types are full hydraulic drives according to the UIC (International Union of Railways) definition, because there is always a fluid circuit in operation. Certain other turbo drives, such as the Lysholm–Smith, have the high speed end of the range operated through an ordinary friction clutch with the converter idling, and so are hydro-mechanical. For purposes of its own when mileage and failure statistics were under review, the British Railways Board (BRB)—successor to the BTC—central mechanical engineering department sometimes excluded Mekydro from the hydraulic category and dubbed it hydro-mechanical.

Power absorption capacity of a turbo converter goes up with the fifth power of the diameter and with the cube of the rotational speed. Locomotive structural considerations limit the diameter; so to get a powerful converter within small diameter, step-up gears are interposed between the engine

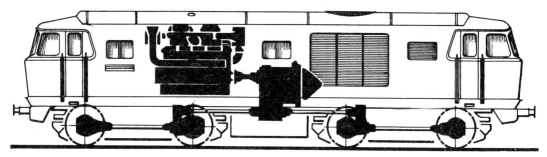

Fig 2 *Skeleton equipment diagram of single-engine B-B diesel-hydraulic locomotive*

crankshaft and the primary shaft of the transmission. With around 1500rpm engine speed, as on the WR, a converter speed around 3000rpm can be obtained conveniently. These step-up gears mean that hydraulic transmission can be driven equally well by quick running or slow running oil engines without transmission weight being affected. The same does not apply in general to diesel-electric propulsion, where step-up gears between engine and generator are comparatively rare.

At the output end of the hydraulic converter further gears give a speed reduction; and then, in double-bogie locomotives as used on the WR, cardan shafts with universal couplings or joints transmit the torque to final bevel gears on the driven axles, sometimes through an intermediate set of gears. In twin-engine locomotives each hydraulic transmission block is on the locomotive frame above the bogie pivot, and cardan shafts are short; no separate distribution gear is then needed. In single-engine B-B locomotives the transmission block is near the centre of the locomotive, and longer cardans lead forward and backward to a distribution box on each bogie. This type of drive is inherent in diesel-hydraulic bogie locomotives; though at times it brings a multiplicity of cardans and straight spur and bevel gears, it ensures the axles in a bogie are mechanically connected, and so the locomotive is less liable to slip than a conventional diesel-electric locomotive with individual axle-hung motors.

This profusion of gears helps to make the transmission efficiency between engine output and axles no higher, and often fractionally lower, than that of electric transmission, say 81/83 per cent peak with electric and 80/81 per cent with hydraulic. In neither instance do these peaks extend over more than a small proportion of the speed and power range; rarely with either transmission can full engine power be applied over the whole track speed range above the adhesion limit.

The *inefficiency* of any transmission system appears somewhere as heat, and this must be dissipated. For a given power and equal inefficiency the heat from hydraulic drive can be dissipated more conveniently, for it is contained mainly in the oil, which itself can be cooled quickly and easily in a heat exchanger tied in to the main radiator circuit. With electric transmission the heat of inefficiency builds up in the copper of the main generator and traction motors, and must be dissipated by air; owing to the mass and nature of rotors and stators this needs electrically-driven motor blowers.

With either transmission the heat to be dissipated is greatest with high tractive efforts at low track speeds. Compared with the engine cooling system the extra needed for transmission oil is 20/25 per cent increase in radiator and fan capacity plus a relatively small heat exchanger adjacent to the hydraulic block. This facility for cooling oil, even through long periods of uphill running at low speed and high tractive effort, gives hydraulic transmission the advantage of high continuous rated tractive effort from a low speed, a considerable advantage for working over the South Devon gradients. Heavy loads could be hauled steadily uphill, even restarted from signal stops and gradually accelerated up the steepest sections, without overheating the transmission oil, by locomotives that could run fast on the easier grades east of Newton Abbot. Such performance was not practicable with the same 2000bhp and electric transmissions then (1955–56) being offered.

These important railway factors were not lost on WR management. As a result, the first Swindon-built D800 B–B diesel-hydraulics of 78½ tons all-on weight had a continuous rated

Table III—Tractive effort characteristics of diesel-hydraulic and diesel-electric locos

Class	Loco all-on weight	Adhesion weight, all-on	Top designed speed	Starting tractive effort at 30% adhesion	Contin. rated wheel-rim te (lb) at speed (mph)	Contin. rated wheel-rim te as % adhesion, and corresponding speed as % of top speed	
	tons	tons	mph	lb			
WR D600	117.4	80	90	53,800	39,600 @ 12.6	22	@ 14
WR D6300-5	68	68	75	45,750	23,900 @ 10.4	15.8	@ 13.9
WR D6306-57	65	65	75	43,600	30,000 @ 8.0	20.5	@ 10.6
WR D800-2	78.6	78.6	90	52,600	43,800 @ 11.8	24.9	@ 13.1
WR D803-32 & 866-70	78.6	78.6	90	52,600	45,000 @ 11.5	25.5	@ 12.8
WR D833-65	80.8	80.8	90	55,000	37,000 @ 14.0	20.5	@ 15.6
WR D7000	75.4	75.4	90	50,200	33,950 @ 12.5	20.1	@ 13.9
WR D1000	108	108	90	72,500	45,200 @ 14.5	18.6	@ 16.1
K-M (DB) ML3000	101	101	87	67,800	59,500 @ 12.3	24.6	@ 14.1
BR D1	138	115	90	70,000	41,000 @ 16.5	13.9	@ 18.3
BR D200	133	108	90	52,000[1]	30,900 @ 19.0	12.8	@ 21.1
BR D1500	115	115	95	62,000[1]	30,000 @ 27.0	11.85	@ 31.5

[1] Limited deliberately to under 30%

wheel-rim tractive effort well above 40,000lb at 12mph for the 90mph top designed speed common to all type 4 diesels. The concurrent D200-class 1Co–Co1 diesel-electrics of 2000bhp had a corresponding value of 30,900lb at 19mph on 133 tons of locomotive weight and 108 tons adhesion weight. Starting tractive effort at 30 per cent adhesion of the D200 was 72,500lb contrasted with the 53,000lb of the diesel-hydraulic, but this was far above coupling strength, and by 10mph the value was below that of the diesel-hydraulic. Table III gives the tractive effort values of all WR diesel-hydraulics and of the BR type 4 diesel-electrics of the time.

When efforts were being made by the WR to attain good power:weight ratios for all trains to speed up the whole system, both the locomotive weight and the coach tare were seen to contribute their quotas. Locomotive values were helped by hydraulic transmission being lighter than electric for any given engine power and top track speed. Investigation of practice as it was when the large BR orders were being placed before 1960 showed that in the power range of 2000/2300bhp, savings of 6 to 7 tons in transmission weight could be made in C–C locomotives, and up to 10 or 15 tons in an 80-ton B–B diesel-hydraulic of 2270bhp over a 133-ton 2000bhp 1Co–Co1 diesel-electric. One BR diesel-electric with a single 850rpm engine of 2300bhp showed a transmission weight of 24 tons against under 9 tons of a diesel-hydraulic of equal output and two 1500 rpm engines. The spread taken from actual weights of non-American locomotives running or under construction over the years 1955–59 is shown in Fig 3.

Values of this order attracted the WR management. With a 375-ton trailing load of express passenger stock to be lifted up the South Devon 1 in 37/50 gradients at as quick a steady speed as could be obtained without piloting, a 78-ton diesel-hydraulic of 2270bhp gave 5.0bhp/ton of moving weight; the 138-ton 2300bhp 1Co–Co1 diesel-electric gave 4.5bhp/ton, and the 133-ton 2000bhp 1Co–Co1 gave 3.95bhp/ton. Put another way, a 78-ton locomotive absorbed about 360hp in getting itself up a 1 in 100 grade at 37mph, whereas a more bulky 138-ton machine required around 500hp; to that extent 140 more dbhp were available from the lighter machine.

As to price, the quoted and accepted cost of two 1100bhp 1500rpm engines, hydraulic transmissions, cardan shafts, axle drives and electric multiple-unit control, *including* 15 per cent import duty, was eight per cent less than the price paid for one home-built slow-speed 2300bhp engine with electric transmission and controls for

Fig 3 *Weight chart of electric and hydraulic transmissions, 1955-59*

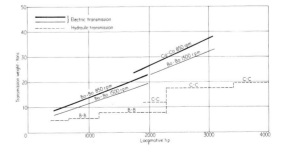

Hymek D7022 shunting tank wagons at Cranmore,
Somerset, in 1966

Ivo Peters

a 1Co–Co1. This price differential was maintained some years later for two home-built 1380 bhp 1500rpm engines and hydraulic drives compared with one 2750bhp slow-speed engine with electric drive, both for six-wheel bogie locomotives; moreover service experience did not show a necessity for derating the quick running engines, whereas the slow-speed type had to be brought down to 2500bhp.

When decisions were being made in 1955–56 the WR management visualised continuous brakes on freight trains as an early and vital part of the modernisation plan, and at that time no consideration was given to dynamic braking of the locomotive. With both systems of transmission such braking was possible, in diesel-electrics by the wheels driving the motors as generators and feeding the generated current to resistance banks, and in diesel-hydraulics by the provision of a special braking converter, the generated heat from which was cooled in extra radiator elements. For most British gradients and loads development of these braking systems was not urgent if continuous brakes were to be fitted to freight stock. In any case, the weight range of diesel locomotives was scarcely taken into account by the operating department, whose basis was simply the weight that could be held on any given gradient by a 20/25-ton goods brake van.

The two-engine principle is not inherent in diesel-hydraulic locomotives. It arose in Britain first because of North British Locomotive Co's ability to build in its own works all three portions for such locomotives (D600 class), and then from the WR's own adoption of the German V200 as the basic model. The twin-engine principle gave possibilities of getting home if one engine failed,

and did just that on the first public demonstration of any diesel-hydraulic on the WR.

A diesel locomotive of any type has several auxiliaries taking power before the transmission input, such as water pumps, oil pumps, and some means of fan drive. Cooling fans absorb some 60hp at full load in a 2000bhp locomotive; the dynastarter will take briefly up to 50 hp and more generally 20 to 30hp in furnishing current to the motors of brake compressors and exhausters, in charging the battery, supplying current to the lighting and control systems, and in winter to the train heating boiler controls. All these are not on at full blast at one time; nevertheless a 2000bhp locomotive will have a reduction of 90/100hp in normal service, so that input to transmission will not be above 1900hp. Transmission efficiency of 80 per cent brings this down to 1525hp at the rail, but that amount is available in a diesel-hydraulic locomotive more or less all the way up the speed range from the continuous rating speed.

Power available at the drawhook is less by the amount absorbed in propelling the locomotive itself, and that is unaffected by the type of transmission. Proportion of drawbar horsepower (dbhp) to rail horsepower (rhp) in a diesel is greater than that with steam, and is governed by the number and arrangement of axles and by the bulk and shape, and is not in direct proportion to the weight. A 138-ton diesel-electric is 70 per cent heavier than an 80-ton diesel-hydraulic, but at any given speed along the level does not absorb 70 per cent more power in propelling itself; the increment is more like 20/25 per cent. Uphill, however, quite different ratios prevail, for the resistance due to gravity is in direct relation to the weight.

CHAPTER 4

BEGINNINGS ON THE WESTERN REGION

THE first Paddington recommendation that diesel-hydraulic locomotives be tried on the WR needed BTC approval, and initially this was given only on a limited scale. Feeling was that any business done by a nationalised transport undertaking with Germany, where the type had been developed, might be a political embarrassment, for the electrical industry's parliamentary and Marylebone lobbies were strong. On the other hand, a proposition to buy diesel-electrics from the USA was given open support in the House by at least one MP; the BTC chairman had visited the EMD factory of General Motors during a trip to the States, and favourable spread-over payment terms had been proposed by at least one American manufacturer.

On prestige grounds adoption by a state system of foreign equipment might not be seemly, first on the grounds of easily stirred mass emotion, and secondly from the viewpoint of British railway headquarters, coming, as it would, only a comparatively short time after a reply had been given in the House of Commons that BR knew all there was to be known about diesel railcar design. Thus, when early in 1955 the WR wanted to obtain serious proposals for diesel-hydraulics, the only manufacturer that could be approached was the North British Locomotive Co Ltd (NBL), which had a Voith transmission licence; in fact BTC approval of the diesel-hydraulic *idea* was held up until a formal offer had been submitted by NBL.

Partly because of the enthusiasm and push of one of the senior technical staff, the late R. H. Fett, NBL around 1948 decided to go into the diesel locomotive business, more than 20 years after the first suggestions. Though diesel locomotives of all types were envisaged, NBL never contemplated making electrical equipment, but to enable more of the whole locomotive to be made in the two Glasgow factories, Fett recommended that a licence be taken for the manufacture of Voith hydraulic drive. This was done in 1951, and involved not only the agreement with Voith but the taking over from the Hydraulic Coupling & Engineering Co Ltd of the British rights in Voith converters held by that company since 1937.

In 1954 a licence was taken by NBL to manufacture MAN oil engines of medium speed and quick running types of 100 to 2000bhp, but up to the time of the BR pilot enquiries NBL had not installed this make, and had used mainly Paxman engines up to about 800bhp. The firm enquiries from the BTC on behalf of the WR thus were for power increases of 25 per cent in engine-transmission groups and 250 per cent in locomotive output on anything NBL had built previously; the BTC orders themselves were the first of any moment NBL received for the MAN type of oil engine.

Among the three high-power quick-running diesels then working in German locomotives the MAN was the heaviest in specific weight, and the Voith transmission was rather weightier than the Mekydro, which had its first application in its fully developed form in 1950. Thus NBL was at a disadvantage in trying to meet WR ideas of 2000bhp on four axles and 80 tons all-on weight. However, the matter was settled from without, because the BTC mechanical engineering department dominated the dealings with NBL. Unappreciative of the elements of railway mechanics, and so unable to appraise the operational principles advocated by the WR management, this department pushed through a 12-wheel design of heavyweight construction, and refused responsibility for a four-wheel bogie to carry 40 tons with a 450hp drive on each axle and a top speed of 90mph.

BTC-central idea, when the Commission was considering an order, was simply to try hydraulic transmission as a transmission on a heavyweight locomotive. The whole WR conception was put aside, and a conservative engineering try-out adopted in preference to a modern traffic-shifting solution. The result was a handful of six-axle locomotives topping 117 tons, and another handful of four-axle 68-ton 1000bhp units.

When these large unwanted A1A–A1A machines were seen to be certain, and no British maker showed any signs of offering locomotives of the type required, the WR in the summer of 1955 took a step that proved vital in getting the whole diesel-hydraulic business going in the desired fashion, by coming into direct contact with Maybach Motorenbau, of Friedrichshafen, and then, through that firm, with Krauss-Maffei

Above: *Second of the D600s, and second WR diesel-hydraulic in service, D601* Ark Royal *with a Paddington–Penzance express at Iver in June 1960*
Derek Cross

Above right: *First Swindon-built diesel-hydraulic D800* Sir Brian Robertson, *and first type 4 diesel built in BR workshops, on a special train before taking up regular service*
British Railways

Below: *German V200.008, model for the WR D800 class, leaves Frankfurt Hauptbahnhof on an FD train*
Deutsche Bundesbahn

(K-M) and the mechanical engineering department of the DB. Maybach had supplied both engines and transmissions of 1000/1100bhp for the V80 and V200 classes on the DB. K-M had designed and built the mechanical portions and erected the locomotives, and held the few relevant patents in the stressed-skin construction and particular type of bogie in the V200 class, the whole conception of which was due largely to the DB diesel traction chief of 1948–54, Curt Lampe.

Maybach assured the WR that the ideas of having an English version of the V200 were quite practical and presented no insuperable technical difficulties. In fact, the firm enlarged the scope by showing that the system of standard and interchangeable engine and transmission parts as then practised at Friedrichshafen could give

locomotives from 800 to 3000bhp in which most wearing parts and many other constituents in the power-transmission plants would be largely the same, and that the methods of mechanical portion design and construction could be maintained in all. Moreover, figures were produced to show that up to August 1955 the five V200 locomotives introduced between December 1953 and April 1954 had accumulated over $1\frac{1}{4}$ million km, and that the monthly distances were rising.

An impressive part of the German V200 conception was the ability to install at will any of three makes of engines and either of two makes of transmission without alteration to the mechanical portion or to such auxiliaries as cooling equipment. Though the three engine makes were of much the same bulk and ran at top speeds around 1500rpm, they varied by 25 per cent in specific weight and were quite different in their principles of design and in their details; but the DB had got together the three engine and two transmission makers, and insisted on common mountings, fuel, oil and water connections, air intakes, and exhaust systems.

From 1956–57 it was not only common to see MAN, Daimler-Benz and Maybach engines coupled indiscriminately to Voith or Mekydro transmissions, but also to see different combinations in one twin-engine locomotive, for example a Maybach engine and Voith drive at one end and a Daimler-Benz engine and Mekydro drive at the other.

This, and the standard engine-transmission components over a wide range of engine output, gave the WR the practical basis it had been seeking for a system-wide application of diesel power, and led it also to consider whether such ideas could be implemented entirely with British manufacture, for BTC objections to foreign-built

equipment on prestige, political and pressure grounds remained.

Here the Germans provided solutions that satisfied the BTC. Maybach offered a competitive price for six engine-transmission-cardan shaft-axle drive-control groups for three twin-engine 2000bhp locomotives, and agreed that if these proved satisfactory, and the WR wished to extend the principle, a search would be made for a British licensee for engine manufacture and, if required, for Mekydro manufacture also. The nature and size of the locomotive superstructure and the more restricted British loading gauge did not permit a competitive cif (cost including freight) offer for a few complete locomotives or mechanical portions, but K-M was willing to grant a licence for manufacture to the BTC and provide drawings and the initial expert advice and collaboration. As this would provide work for railway workshops to counter diminishing steam locomotive activity, it was accepted, and some intensive work was done to get a mutually satisfactory agreement through quickly so that Swindon could begin construction.

Apart from down payments that could amount to over £200 per locomotive, there was a sliding scale of licence fees per locomotive built, which began at DM17,640/locomotive for the first 10, DM14,700/locomotive for Nos 11 to 25, until a final fee of DM4410/locomotive from No 101 upwards. Should K-M itself make any parts for the BTC the fee would be reduced. This agreement was signed at a time when the rate of exchange was about DM11.2 to £1; in all 145 diesel-hydraulics were built under the licence.

Introduction of the WR to the DB led to the provision of much detailed information as to traffic performance, working diagrams, maintenance and reliability, and to preliminary visits of

D801 Vanguard, *one of the first three Swindon-built Warships of 2070bhp begins the climb up the Kennet valley from Reading West in 1959; note the old style headcode panel*

M. W. Earley

WR and BTC technical staff to K-M and to DB repair shops and depots to examine schedules, equipment, driving and training methods relevant to the V200 and the smaller single-engine (1000bhp) V80 classes; and to Friedrichshafen to gain some knowledge of the details of engines and transmissions.

In the autumn of 1955 discussions took place at Paddington as to the possibility of building a handful of fast fixed-formation diesel-hydraulic train sets using engines and transmissions absolutely standard with those it was proposed to order for German-type locomotives. In view of the opposition to the whole diesel-hydraulic project, and similar objections to other WR proposals, Grand and Phillips were unwilling to force the subject further at that time; in the event, the same winter, a BTC internal commission took up the idea using diesel-electric propulsion which developed into the diesel blue Pullman trains.

The three initial locomotives ordered from Swindon in January 1956 to absorb the six power-transmission-control sets to come from Maybach were part of the pilot scheme. They were also the thin end of a wedge that opened the door for diesel-hydraulics wider than the diesel-electric-minded BTC central mechanical engineering department thought necessary or desirable, for naturally the BTC financial authorities did not

want to see the down payments to K-M and high initial licence fees spread over a bare handful of locomotives; nor did the more practical elements at the Commission feel enough work had been produced for the railway shops if only three units were built.

As recorded in chapter 1, the locomotive part of the modernisation plan was stepped up considerably in 1957–58, and the pilot scheme went by the board. As a forerunner of the accelerated programme the BTC sanctioned in February 1957 the construction at Swindon of another 30 diesel-hydraulics similar to the three then building, and in view of the urgent situation agreed that the power-transmission-control equipments should be supplied by Maybach. The order brought the WR more into line with the other regions, all of which except the Southern had many more diesel locomotives coming forward from the pilot scheme, but the order also put the WR far ahead of any other region in the number of type 4 locomotives on order.

This was the event that led to the beginning of powerful opposition to diesel-hydraulics on the part of the British electrical and oil engine industries and of the BTC mechanical engineering department. While there seemed no likelihood of more than a handful of diesel-hydraulics, no opposition was necessary, particularly as all, or nearly all, the work could be expected by the one large locomotive builder who was already in the diesel-electric stream; but a forceful entry by a foreign maker was a different matter. From that time forward strong efforts were made to publicise hydraulic transmission as well suited to shunting and trip-train working but for nothing else, and that there was no experience with it in high powers. This view neglected the 55 successful V200 locomotives of the DB which by 1957 were building up monthly mileages greater than those of any European diesel-electrics, from 12,000 to 15,000 miles per locomotive in 30 days.

Among the spate of orders placed by the BTC through 1957–59 was that for 52 type 2 diesel-hydraulics in November 1957, and another in July 1958 for a further 33 diesel-hydraulics of the German, or D800, class. To assist quicker delivery in view of Swindon's commitments on the preceding 33 units, and to still any internal and external ripples about 'buying German', both orders were given to NBL on the understanding that the greater majority, if not all, of the engines and transmissions would be built in Glasgow. That meant the engines would be of MAN type and the transmissions Voith; the 33 type 4 locomotives with this equipment would equal the three prototypes and 30 later locomotives of Maybach-Mekydro type being built at Swindon. Interchange of power-transmission equipment was stipulated. The last of the NBL locomotives was not put into traffic until June 1962, by which time the company was facing voluntary liquidation.

Fabrication by NBL was possible because under pressure from the BTC a licence had been granted to NBL by K-M in 1957, to cover locomotives of 2000bhp upwards for the United Kingdom; only a small adjustment to the terms was needed in 1958. The complete manufacturing drawings were sent from Swindon to NBL as representing the English-dimensioned revised design.

To make up the full 70 or so type 4 diesel-hydraulics envisaged at the beginning for the No 1 conversion scheme, a final order for five more Maybach-Mekydros was placed at Swindon in April 1959, and these (D866–70) followed through the works the preceding D803–32 , and were delivered in the summer of 1961.

Meanwhile Maybach investigated the business of a British licensee, and signed an agreement in April 1958 with Bristol Siddeley Engines (BSE) for the manufacture of MD–type engines. Later a licence to make Mekydro transmissions and Maybach axle drives was concluded with Stone-Platt Industries, manufacture to be done at the Deptford and Charlton works of J. Stone & Co.

These activities, and probable further big BTC business, coupled with the finale of the Beyer-Garratt steam locomotive in new construction, attracted Beyer-Peacock (B-P) the Manchester-based locomotive builders. Hitherto, apart from the joint establishment with Metro-Vick of a smallish works at Stockton-on-Tees to erect straight electric and diesel-electric locomotives, its diesel work had been limited to acting as subcontractor for mechanical portions of some of the Brush type 2 diesel-electrics for BR. When BTC enquiries for powerful mixed-traffic diesels were seen to be imminent, B-P, BSE and Stone set up a joint company, Beyer Peacock (Hymek) Ltd which tendered successfully for what came to be known as the Hymek locomotives.

Construction of this single-engine type was permitted by Maybach's development of a 16-cylinder engine, and the introduction of a Mekydro of 1800hp input capacity. Though the UIC rating of this engine was 2000 metric bhp at 1500rpm, a setting of 1740 British bhp was deemed sufficient for WR duties. Most of the equipment was licence-built in England, and many of the engine moving and wearing parts were standard with the engines in the D800 class.

The way for the final and largest development of WR diesel-hydraulics was also opened up by standard engine and transmission developments, but here Maybach-type engines made in England were combined with Voith transmissions made largely in Glasgow. Adoption of charge-air cooling had raised the rated output of the 12-cylinder Maybach engine to 1500 metric bhp. When more power was needed on the WR two of these revised engines were installed as the power portion of the D1000-class design, but were set to 1380bhp apiece, making 2760bhp total, which suited the new Voith transmission of 1300hp input capacity.

The whole of the WR line-service diesel locomotive requirements could be covered by one make of engine with standard cylinders and other details throughout three models, and by one make of transmission in two models; but to give a spread through industry two makes of engines and two types of transmissions were adopted in practice. The common standard mountings and connections gave a potential flexibility in installation that was never fully utilised on the WR as it was on the DB.

CHAPTER 5

ENGINES AND TRANSMISSIONS

WITH the exception of two Paxmans, May-bach and MAN engines of both German and British manufacture were the sole power in WR diesel-hydraulic locomotives. As recorded in chapter 4, each maker had its own British licensee, BSE and NBL respectively. BSE engines were built in a post-war factory at Ansty, near Coventry, but much of the small component machining was done at the adjacent Parkside works. NBL engines were made at Springburn. In both cases such specialised accessories as fuel pumps were obtained from outside works.

All WR Maybach engines were in the MD range in 12- and 16-cylinder models. All MAN-type engines were 12-cylinder models, basically the L12V18/21, but with two suffix letters denoting variations. One D800-class locomotive, D830, was fitted with two Paxman Ventura engines built at Colchester, with the idea of giving a trial to British-conceived power. All engines were pressure-charged. Of the total installed WR power of 602,870bhp in 459 engines mounted in 309 locomotives, 323 Maybach

engines aggregated 454,890bhp in 212 loco-motives, 134 MAN engines totalled 145,800bhp in 96 locomotives, and two Paxman engines gave 2270bhp in one locomotive. Of the 323 Maybach engines, 74 were model MD650, 148 were model MD655, and 101 were model MD870. These were the totals referred to by locomotive; spare Maybach and MAN engines brought the total number up to about 490 and the aggregate bhp to around 639,500.

Confusion as to engine power settings has sometimes been caused by Maybach's use of metric bhp and BR and WR use of British hp. One metric hp is 0.983 of a British hp, and the Maybach MD650 engine's UIC rating of 1200 bhp was equivalent to 1180 British bhp. The British Standard rating for oil engines was some-what different from the UIC norms, principally in catering for different humidity and altitude; though every engine model had its own value, the BS rating in British hp was usually about 0.96 of the UIC rating in metric hp. Unless specifically stated otherwise, hp values given

Right: Fig 4 *Cross-section through Maybach MD870 engine*

Below: *Maybach MD 870 engine of the type installed in the Hymek locomotives; full rated output 2000bhp at 1500rpm; horizontal cylinder in foreground is the heat exchanger for cooling of lubricating oil*

Motoren und Turbinen Union

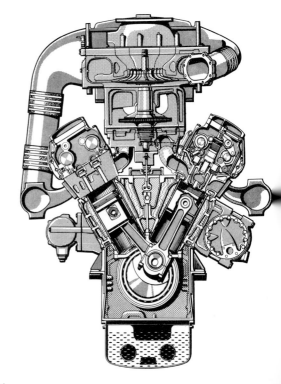

Table IV—Characteristics of diesel engines as used in WR diesel-hydraulic locomotives

Make and model	PC or[1] IC	No of cyls	bhp[2]	Cylinder dimensions mm (in)	rpm	Corresp. brake mean pressure lb/sq in	Dry weight lb	Dry weight lb/bhp	Piston speed ft/min	Output per litre of swept volume bhp
Maybach MD650	PC	12	1135	185 x 200 (7.3 x 7.9)	1530	150	10,250	9.05	2015	17.6
Maybach MD655	IC	12	1380	185 x 200 (7.3 x 7.9)	1500	184	10,875	7.85	1975	21.4
Maybach MD870	IC	16	1740	185 x 200 (7.3 x 7.9)	1500	174	15,000	8.65	1975	20.25
MAN L12V18/21A	PC	12	1000	180 x 210 (7.1 x 8.3)	1445	140	8500	8.5	1995	15.6
MAN L12V18/21B	PC	12	1100	180 x 210 (7.1 x 8.3)	1530	146	9000	8.2	2115	17.2
Paxman 12YJX	PC	12	1135	197 x 216 (7.75 x 8.5)	1530	122	7850	6.92	2165	14.2

[1] PC = Pressure-charged; IC = Pressure-charged and intercooled   [2] Brake horsepower, WR setting

hereafter are in British (*not* BS) units. Basic technical particulars of the engines used on the WR are given in Table IV, and their settings in WR locomotives in Table V.

A wide power range was covered by Maybach engines having the same moving and wearing parts, first by the two different cylinder numbers and, secondly, by the addition of charge-air cooling to the normal pressure-charging thus giving an increase of 10 to 25 per cent in engine output. A pressure-charger is simply a single-stage gas turbine coupled direct to a single-stage centrifugal air compressor, in which the turbine is driven by the engine exhaust gas before it goes out to atmosphere. All today are on principles evolved by the late A. J. Büchi, and perfected in collaboration between him and Brown Boveri in Switzerland. The Maybach turbo-charger differed from all others in its vertical shaft arrangement, adopted deliberately for traction installations to occupy space in the roof not otherwise utilised.

Maybach's engine code numbers provided no indication of the number of cylinders, but gave a close approximation to the total piston-swept volume. Thus the 12-cylinder model MD650 was close on 65 litres volume; the charge-air cooled version with the same swept volume was MD655. The 16-cylinder pressure-charged model MD865 had a swept volume a little over 86 litres, and the charge-air cooled version was MD870. All MD engines were V type with a 60° angle between the two cylinder banks; in all the cylinder bore was 185mm and the piston stroke 200mm (7.3in by 7.9in). The MD was a post-war design with a tunnel crankcase, housing a crankshaft whose circular webs were encased in roller bearings that formed the main shaft supports; the outer races were in the transverse stiffeners of the crankcase. This gave great rigidity to the whole rotating mass and to the engine frame.

Use of the crankwebs for the main bearings gave more space for the crankpins, and the big-end unit bearing load could thus be made low and the piston thrust well distributed over tri-metal plain bearings in the fork-and-blade connecting rods. Corollaries were the short engine length, scarcely 7ft for 2000bhp, and the short cylinder-centre distance. The whole engine design specifically was to combine high speed and high pres-

Table V—Diesel engines used in WR diesel-hydraulic locomotives

Make and Model	WR loco class	UIC rating (metric bhp)[1] and speed (rpm)	British Standard rating (British bhp) and speed (rpm)	WR setting (British bhp) and speed (rpm)
Maybach MD650	D800	1200 @ 1500	1150 @ 1500	1135 @ 1530
Maybach MD655	D1000	1500 @ 1500	1440 @ 1500	1380 @ 1500
Maybach MD870	D7000	2000 @ 1500	1920 @ 1500	1740 @ 1500
MAN L12V18/21A	D600	1075 @ 1500	1000 @ 1445	1000 @ 1445
MAN L12V18/21B	D800	1100 @ 1500	1056 @ 1500	1100 @ 1530
Paxman 12YJX	D830	1250 @ 1500	1200 @ 1500	1135 @ 1530

[1] One metric np = 0.983 British hp

Mekydro K104 transmission of 1035hp input (left) and K184 model of 1800hp input (right); output flanges can be seen below in the carrying frame. Torque converter casing at the near end in each model

Motoren und Turbinen Union

Lowering the disc-webbed crankshaft and its main roller bearings into the crankcase of a Maybach 16-cylinder MD engine

Motoren und Turbinen Union

sures, to get a high power engine on light weight and within restricted bulk while retaining the big distances between overhauls. To maintain high rating the MD engine had a two-piece piston, the detachable top (or hot) portion being of steel. This was cooled by pump circulation of oil separate from the general lubrication system. Another feature was a unit injector for each cylinder, which combined in one assembly a fuel pump ram and an injector, so there was no large single multi-ram pump for the whole engine.

Construction of the MD range from 1000 to 2000bhp per engine was based on the machining of standard parts and erection into interchangeable sub-assemblies. The 16-cylinder engine installed in the Hymek locomotives, for example, had 6500 separate parts including every set screw, split pin, nut, etc; but as many parts, such as the valve springs, were the same throughout, there were only 860 different scheduled items. Of this number about 260 were special to the 16-cylinder engine; the balance of 600, representing about 4900 single parts, was standard with all other models. Thus about 75 per cent of all parts in a 16-cylinder engine were repetitive.

Detailed improvements always had mountings or connections interchangeable with the part replaced. Until 1956–57 all the 12-cylinder engines had cast iron crankcases and engine frame structures. When the 16-cylinder model was

developed a fabricated structure of steel plates, steel castings and drop forgings was introduced as better suited to the greater length, though it was 30 per cent lighter than a cast iron frame. Then when the MD650 engine was developed into the charge-air cooled MD655, and the rated output increased 25 per cent, a fabricated crankcase-engine-frame was adopted, following 16-cylinder practice. Subsequently, for production reasons, this was applied to all 12-cylinder engines.

The MAN-type engines were of altogether simpler character; they were the conventional form developed to its maximum possibility—perhaps beyond it. All installed by the WR were the same basic L12V18/21 model; the first figure gave the number of cylinders, and the other two the cylinder bore and piston stroke in cm, that is 180mm by 210mm. This MAN engine underwent certain detail developments around 1956–57. The first supplied to the WR for locomotives D600–4 and D6300–5 were the older L12V18/21A model; the remainder, beginning in 1959, were the revised L12V18/21B. The code L12V18/21S was used sometimes by NBL, the S for supercharged taking the place of the German A for Aufladung.

Crankcase and cylinder blocks were of mild steel with cast steel transversals welded up as one piece for the whole engine, with an angle of 60°

between the two banks and a flat stiffener across the top of the V. Dry weight was approximately 8500lb for the earlier engines and 9000lb for the later deliveries. Only one camshaft, in the neck of the V, was used to actuate all 48 valves (two inlet and two exhaust valves per cylinder), and the low location involved a smaller gear train for the drive from the crankshaft than found in the Maybach engine with its four overhead camshafts. Two six-ram fuel injection pumps were mounted in tandem above the V in the early engines; they were of CAV make in Glasgow-built engines. Connecting rods were plain, two being arranged side by side on each crankpin, which meant that opposite cylinders were slightly staggered. No piston cooling was provided.

From 1958 injection pumps were mounted side by side on the flat deck above the neck of the V, with the governor at the driving end; pistons were changed to forged aluminium alloy from the cast type, and the top piston ring was chrome plated; crankpin diameter was increased from 118mm to 125mm; when rated speed was put up from 1400/1445rpm to 1500/1530rpm a sleeve-spring vibration damper was fitted to the free end of the crankshaft; only one exhaust manifold per cylinder bank was used in place of two, and a helix was inserted to keep the exhaust pulses separate until they reached the pressure-charger branch; the big ends were split diagonally and given serrated matching faces in place of the old plain-faced joint. These changes brought the L12V18/21B engine.

Early L12V18/21A engines on the WR had a railway rating of 1000bhp at 1445rpm; 1100bhp at 1500rpm was considered then as no more than a one-hour output. The revised L12V18/21B model was given a railway rating of 1100bhp at 1530 rpm following experience with the revised details and a DB 80-hr continuous test run at that output. The equivalent brake mean pressure (bmp) in the cylinders at 1100bhp and 1500rpm was 146 lb/sq in. This was a high figure for a conventional engine without piston cooling, and may have been the origin of some of the troubles encountered.

Paxman 12YJX engines installed in locomotive D830 had a BS rating of 1200bhp at 1500rpm, but to correspond with the other makes in the rest of the D800s they were set to 1135 bhp at 1530rpm. This was a comparatively simple design of 60° V, lightweight but not highly rated. Like the MAN it had a welded steel frame with cast steel transversals, but unlike the MAN its fuel pumps were outside the cylinders, not

between. Cylinders were 7.75in by 8.5in. Alone among all types it had two more main bearings than the number of crank throws, a second one having been added at the driving end to help in supporting the weight of any heavy driven member such as the armature of an electric generator.

Among ancillaries the cooling equipment is the most important. It is in the form of radiator banks in or near the side walls, through which air is sucked by a roof-mounted fan and expelled upwards. The fan operates under thermostatic control governed by the water temperature at the engine exit, so that the greater the engine load and the higher the water temperature the faster is the fan speed. By this means, whatever the engine load up to its maximum, the cooling water is kept within a narrow temperature range.

In WR locomotives D600–4 and D6300–5 the fan was driven by an electric motor, the speed of which was varied by a thermostat in the engine water circuit. With the Swindon-built prototype D800 was introduced the Behr system, in which the fan was driven by a small high pressure hydrostatic swash-plate motor fed from an engine driven hydrostatic pump of the same construction as the motor, and the oil delivery from which was under thermostatic control. Equipment in these locomotives also included movable shutters outside the radiator banks, operated by small hydraulic cylinders. The hydrostatic pump was driven by a cardan shaft from the engine (D800 class and D6306–57) or from a transmission shaft (D1000 and D7000 classes). Beginning with the Behr equipments, complete cooling units could be lowered into and lifted out of the locomotive in one piece.

When the engine was started and idled the pump circulation of the water through the radiator was enough to keep the temperature within bounds without the fan turning. When the driver's control handle was moved to the first power notch the fan began to move and the shutters began to open. Thereafter, as power was increased, the fan speed rose and the shutters opened wider. Usually the thermostatic control was set to begin operation around 78/80°C, to bring the engine back to idling if water temperature rose beyond 88/90°C, and to cut out the thermostatic action if, under light load or closing the throttle to idling, the water exit temperature fell to 75°C. In normal working the fan speed and quantity of air passed were varying most of the time by reason of the changing engine load from variations in gradient and track speed. The shutters also fulfilled the minor function

Left: *Behr-Serck cooling unit comprising side radiator blocks and removable shutters, with frame and header tank; high-pressure hydrostatic pipes and pump within*

British Railways

of helping to prevent a freeze-up during a winter night's lie-over, but that could be prevented absolutely by a small oil-fired heater inserted in a bypass of the engine water system, so that the water could be preheated to prevent any dead-cold start, and which could be kept on for long period at trifling cost to prevent any freezing in the circuit. Another desirable although not essential engine safeguard fitted was that when the engine starting switch was turned it set to work first an electrically-driven oil priming pump, and only when this had built up a certain pressure in the lubricating circuit did the dynastarter come into action and start the engine.

Engine water was not the only fluid that had to be cooled. Lubricating oil also had to be dealt with, and also the oil of the hydraulic transmission. Both were covered by the common water circuit which flowed through the main radiators. In the MD655 and MD870 engines, however, cooling of the charge-air was done in a secondary water circuit which had its own pump and radiator elements. To get both engine and transmission oil up to working levels quickly, these two fluids were passed through heat exchangers, the water side of which was in the main cooling circuit.

Engines of all classes were started electrically by a dynastarter, the name implying the double function of dynamo (current generator) and motor (current user). When operating as a dynamo current was furnished to the electrically driven auxiliaries, lighting and control, and to battery charging. When acting as a motor to start the engine, current was drawn from the battery. The dynastarter was attached by cardan shaft either to the engine crankshaft or to a shaft on the primary side of the transmission.

Distribution of the two hydraulic transmissions on the WR was: Voith aggregating 345,600hp (engine) in 282 sets installed in 170 locomotives, and Mekydro aggregating 257,300hp (engine) in 177 sets installed in 139 locomotives. Of the Voith total 16 sets were model L306r, 118 were LT306r, and 148 were L630rV. Mekydro was divided into 76 sets of model K104 and 101 of model K184. Of the total of 1384 axle drives throughout the WR diesel-hydraulic fleet, 252 in the D600 and D6300 classes were from David Brown; the other 1132 were Maybach type, 486 of model C33 and 646 'of model C33v. Of the Mekydro K104 model all 76 were made at Friedrichshafen, plus another 15 spares; 25 of the K184 were made at Friedrichshafen and 76 by Stone, but Stone also made 15 spare sets. NBL manufacture of Voith transmissions was concentrated at Queen's Park works on the south side of the Clyde. The last few transmissions of

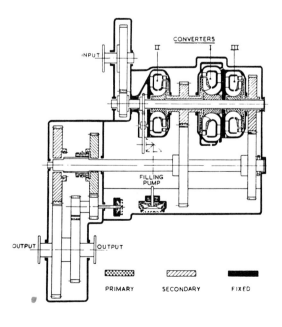

Left: Fig 5 *Schematic section through Voith triple-converter transmission*

Right: Fig 6 *Schematic section
through Mekydro
transmission. Key:*
1–*Turbo converter*
2–*Step-up input gear*
3–*Disengageable converter*
4–*Secondary shaft*
5–*Claw couplings*
6–*Reversing wheels*
7–*Idler from reverse to output
shaft*
8–*Output flange*
9–*Pressure and suction pump*
*a to f–change-speed gear
wheels*

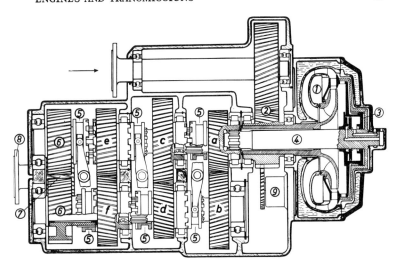

all were made at that works by Voith Engineering (Glasgow) Ltd after NBL had taken steps to go into voluntary liquidation.

All Voith transmissions on the WR were of three-converter form. In D600–4 and D6300–5 model L306r had a maximum input capacity around 950hp which suited the MAN 1000bhp engine then being put in. This model had the output directly below the input, and the short output shaft had two flanges to take cardan shafts going forward and backward. The block as a whole was practically the same in D600–4 and D6300–5, but the latter had an extra external drive line taken from the input step-up gears to the dynastarter, whereas in D600–4 the dynastarter was driven from the free end of the engine crankshaft. The later D6306–57 and D833–65 had a revised model known as LT306r of more compact form and of 1000hp input capacity. Here the dynastarter drive was taken from an extension of the primary shaft of the transmission.

All 74 locomotives of D1000 class had the then new L630rV model of 1270hp input capacity, which made it suitable for the MD655 engine at a reduced output. This was a development from the older L306 models, but coincidentally Voith changed its code-number arrangement. Previously the first digit had been the number of converters, the second the number of fluid couplings, and the third figure the maker's power-size number. From 1961 the first figure gave the power-size number, the second gave the number of converters, and the third the number of fluid couplings. Suffix r meant reversing gears were included within the transmission block, V showed the output was at the bottom of the block, at the opposite end to the input.

Track speeds for the change-over from one converter to another as given in subsequent chapters for the different locomotive classes are approximate only, for the converters changed up at a slightly higher speed than they changed down. In these Voith transmissions the step-up gears led to the main hollow hydraulic shaft on which were fixed the three pump impellers; the three corresponding turbine runners were bolted to a solid secondary shaft that ran through the centre of the hollow primary shaft. Driven by the engine, the impeller part generated kinetic energy in the oil, which impinged on the blades of the runner, and after turning that part was returned to the impeller by blades fixed on the converter casing which took the reaction. The torque produced by whichever turbine runner was in circuit was transmitted by straight spur gears mounted on the solid secondary shaft to an intermediate shaft, and then to the output shaft through a further pair of gears for forward motion or an alternative combination for backward movement. The converter parts always turned in the same direction. With one converter in circuit the impellers in the other two ran idle at whatever speed the converter in use was making.

The three torque converters were of different sizes, oil capacities and blade formations to suit the various requirements; the starting, or high torque, converter was the largest and the high speed low torque converter the smallest. From the hollow primary shaft was taken a small spur and bevel drive to the filling pump that maintained the hydraulic circuits.

The throttle was linked to the transmission so that when the engine was started it idled in zero notch but the transmission was not engaged; on movement to No 1 notch the transmission was switched in and the first converter filled. A single lever on the driving dashboard actuated both engine throttle and transmission filling. Reversing was by a separate handle which could be operated only at standstill. The governor, solenoid, change-over valves, filter and other details were grouped accessibly on one side of the transmission block.

Mekydro, as used on the WR, had one permanently filled converter, three sets of spur gears with over-running claw clutches which gave four gear steps, and the necessary pair of reversing gears. After the step-up gear and the converter were nine straight tooth gears in the transmission block. As with the Voith drive, incorporation of the reversing gears within the transmission casing meant the axle drives need be only of simple bevel form in two-axle bogie locomotives.

Change from one set of gears to another was made automatically according to track speed through the medium of the claw clutches. At the moment of change the turbine blades in the converter were momentarily and automatically disengaged from the hydraulic circuit by a small axial movement. The secondary part of the converter had a further blade ring not in the fluid circuit while the converter was engaged, and gave a weak backward torque when the turbine was briefly withdrawn. By this means synchronisation in gear changes was undertaken by the converter, which actually had a triple function: torque converter, disconnecting coupling, and synchroniser of claw-clutch action.

Drop in tractive effort at a gear change was full but brief, normally only for a fraction of a second. The electrically controlled oil-pressure operated control mechanism was in an interchangeable sub-assembly mounted above the main transmission block. With its numerous small-bore passages, piston-type plungers, flat-seated valves and gear selectors it was complicated to make and assemble.

Mekydro model K104 in D800–3 had a maximum input capacity of 966hp, but altered construction in all the others brought input capacity up to 1035hp. The larger K184U type was put into the Hymek locomotives. In each case the first two figures gave the maximum input capacity in hundreds of hp, and the last figure denoted the number of gear stages. Suffix U represented cardan shaft drive from two output flanges at the bottom. The K104U block with control attachment weighed 4250lb empty and the heat exchanger another 250lb; corresponding weights for the K184U were 8600lb and 530lb.

A summary of the various combinations of the above engines and transmissions in the five major classes of WR diesel-hydraulic locomotives is given in Table VI. Despite interchangeability of mounting and other details there was in practice no interchange of engine and transmission makes to get locomotives back into traffic more quickly.

Table VI—Engines and transmissions in WR diesel-hydraulic locomotives

Loco Class	Engine model	Engine maker	Transmission model	Transmission maker	Engine setting bhp @ rpm
D600-4	MAN L12V18/21A	MAN & NBL	Voith L306r	Voith & NBL	2 x 1000 @ 1445
D6300-5	MAN L12V18/21A	NBL	Voith L306r	NBL	1000 @ 1445
D6306-57	MAN L12V18/21B	NBL	Voith LT306r	Voith & NBL	1100 @ 1530
D800-2	Maybach MD650	Maybach	Mekydro K104U	Maybach	2 x 1035 @ 1400
D803-29, 831-32, 866-70	Maybach MD650	Maybach	Mekydro K104U	Maybach	2 x 1135 @ 1530
D830	Paxman 12YJX	Paxman	Mekydro K104U	Maybach	2 x 1135 @ 1530
D833-65	MAN L12V18/21B	NBL	Voith LT306r	NBL	2 x 1100 @ 1530
D1000-73	Maybach MD655	BSE	Voith L630rU	Voith & NBL	2 x 1380 @ 1500
D7000-100	Maybach MD870	BSE	Mekydro	Maybach & Stone	1740 @ 1500

CHAPTER 6

D600 CLASS

THESE five locomotives, D600–4, were the unblest fruit of BTC mechanical engineering insistence on heavyweight engineering for mechanical portions to house lightweight oil engines and fluid transmissions, married to the inexperience of NBL in large diesel locomotive design and building and in oil engine construction and installation. They could be described as diesel-hydraulics with quick running engines built on the basis of diesel-electrics with slow running heavyweight engines.

Quoted price was £86,000 per locomotive, with the labour and material variation clauses usual in contracts at that period. By the time the last of the five locomotives was completed the authorised additions and alterations had brought the price above £87,500 per locomotive, but this was still a low price for the time at £43.5/bhp and £800/ton of empty weight. In fact it was an undercut price. Drawing office charges alone were £30,000, and spread over only five locomotives meant £6000 a piece, or almost seven per cent of the agreed price. Delivery was promised to begin in 15 months and to be at the rate of one locomotive per month, but this was not approached. Some of the delay was due to requested modifications, delay in approving details, and the second thoughts of the BTC on equipment to be fitted. The D600 price did not include buffers and screw couplings, which were free issue from the BTC.

In the BTC's eyes the D600 was to be the diesel hydraulic equivalent of the 2000 and 2300 bhp diesel-electrics being ordered at the same time, but despite the insistence on heavy weight no excuse could be found for going above six axles, whereas the diesel-electrics needed eight. In contrast the diesel-electrics had six of their eight axles individually driven; the diesel-hydraulics could not be provided with six driven axles because the designers could not think out a pivotless bogie and driving arrangement to suit, and in the summer of 1955 there were no C–C diesel-hydraulic locomotives elsewhere to serve as a model. So the axle notation became A1A–A1A using a cardan shaft layout similar to a B–B, with two axles out of six idling, and those bearing almost 19 tons apiece compared with the 20 tons on each driving axle.

As an engineering try-out of hydraulic drive, which was the BTC reason for construction, the D600 class was unnecessary because the smaller D6300 type ordered concurrently had the same transmission model and was cheaper to build. The D600 resulted from a double yielding to pressure, the WR having to accept the BTC idea of heavyweight and the BTC giving in to WR insistence on at least some diesel-hydraulic prototypes in power class 4. The larger type gave facility for designing and installing controls for two engine-transmission groups in one locomotive, and for four in two locomotives coupled in multiple-unit and driven by one man.

By reason of the great weight and air-braked blocks on all wheels, a braking force of 88 tons could be applied. This was a help in controlling the heavy unbraked freight trains that were no part of the modernisation plan, and which, according to diesel-electric policy, needed six driving axles, though in practice few unbraked freights were handled by the D600s in early years. Continuous rated wheel-rim tractive effort of 39,600lb at 12.6mph with new wheels was equivalent to 22.2 per cent adhesion at 14 per cent of top speed of 90mph; but the adhesion weight itself was only 68 per cent of the locomotive total.

Main equipment was grouped in the superstructure symmetrically about a Spanner train heating boiler, though this item itself was slightly off-centre longitudinally to get a cross passage from one side to the other. Flanking this boiler were, in sequence, a dynastarter, the engine, and the main transmission block, the free end of the last-named being close against the inner bulkhead of the driving cab. In plan the two groups were staggered, one set slightly to the right hand side and the other an equal distance to the left hand side of the longitudinal centre line of the locomotive.

The cooling fans were in the roof above the two transmission blocks, driven under thermostatic control by electric motors. They, too, were offset in plan, but on the opposite sides to the engine-shaft lines, and staggered to suit them. The radiator banks were well within the body, not on the side walls, and each cooling group was in a compartment of its own. Engine exhaust went up through the roof at the transmission end

31

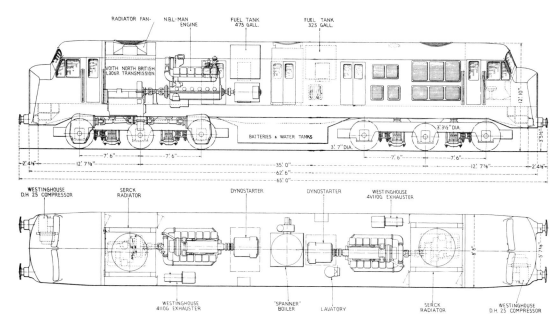

of the engine. Each 35kW dynastarter was driven through a flexible coupling from the engine shaft, and had a control to maintain 110V supply whatever the rotational speed.

Partly because NBL was feeling its way, and partly because of the input capacity of the transmission installed, each of the MAN-type L12V18/21A engines was set to 1000bhp at 1445rpm. As recorded in chapter 5, MAN itself in 1955–56 was busy on detail modifications that were to bring 1100bhp as the normal railway rating. The engines in D600–4 were of the older type with fuel injection pumps set tandemwise and driven off one end of the single camshaft. The engines in D600–1 came from Augsburg; those in D602–4 were Glasgow-built.

A difference between German-built and Glasgow-built engines was the changed ancillaries, so that there was no dependence on European suppliers for equipment and spares; to implement this policy some of the German-built engines were given British ancillaries. Exhaust-gas pressure-chargers were of Napier make in place of MAN; fuel injection pumps were CAV in place of Bosch; Vokes air filters were used instead of Knecht; radiator elements and headers were from Serck in place of Behr; EEC dynastarters replaced the Brown Boveri make; and DP starting batteries were installed in place of AFA.

Each engine drove a Voith model L306r triple-converter transmission through step-up gears above the input end of the main casing. This model had been introduced in Germany in some of the 50 new V200 locomotives set to work in that year. It had input capacities of 927hp at 1445rpm engine speed and 980hp at 1500rpm, and was designed as far as possible to parallel the characteristics of the Mekydro K104 drive that had been installed in the five V200 locomotives of 1953–54, as both makes had to be applied without extraneous change to all future V200 locomotives. The four transmissions for D600–1 were made at Heidenheim; those for D602–4 were built by NBL.

Change-over points of the converters were about 29 and 57mph upwards and 53 and 27mph downwards. The transmission block was above the bogie, and the lower output drive, at the same end as the upper input, was above the centre axle and large pivot. The cardan shafts that went forward and backward to the two end axle drives had equal angles of inclination for any movement of the bogie relative to the body. Axle drives were spiral bevel and helical gear double reduction sets of 2.84:1 ratio. As with the engine, the transmission members from the hydraulic block were of English make.

Basis of the mechanical portion were large rivetted and welded I sections with $\frac{3}{4}$in webs and welded cross stretchers, thick floor plate and cast steel dragboxes. As if to make up for the enormous amount of ferrous material in underframes and bogies, the superstructure, apart from the base angles and roof formers, was of aluminium sections and plates. Each driving cab was

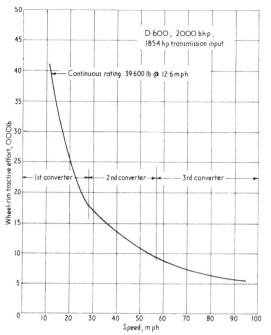

Above: Fig 8 *Speed/tractive effort curve, D600 class*

Left: Fig 7 *General layout of equipment, D600 class*
Railway Gazette and North British Locomotive Co

Below: *Erection of main frame, light alloy cabs, tanks and other details in NBL works*

remarkable for being a single sub-assembly of several Alpax castings welded together on the Argonarc process, and jig-mounted for final assembly. Bare weight of this sub-assembly was 800lb. Corrosion at the steel/aluminium joints at the underframe was prevented by a zinc-chromate primer. Glass fibre insulation was moulded inside the cab. Cab handrails were stainless steel. Light alloy hinged doors were fitted in the cab noses to give gangway passage from one locomotive to another when coupled in tandem. No train indicator panels were included when new; painted number boards were hung on the doors when any train headcode indication was necessary.

Each side member of a bogie frame structure was a welded sub-assembly of two deep plates with ties and stiffening ribs, and the two sub-assemblies were connected by rivetted cross stretchers and headstocks. Superstructure weight was carried on each bogie by two bearers per side, resting on the double swing-link bolster, which had transverse laminated springs suspended from the bogie by swing links and planks. Traction, braking and side thrusts, but no weight, were transmitted above the centre axle through large inner and outer centering rings which also formed the pivot. Inner and outer portions were attached respectively to the underframe and bolster, and the inner ring was large enough to encircle the transmission output gears. Timken roller bearing axleboxes had coil springs bearing on equalising beams and truck frame, and ran in guides with manganese steel liners. This bogie was a good rider, and the D600s were smooth

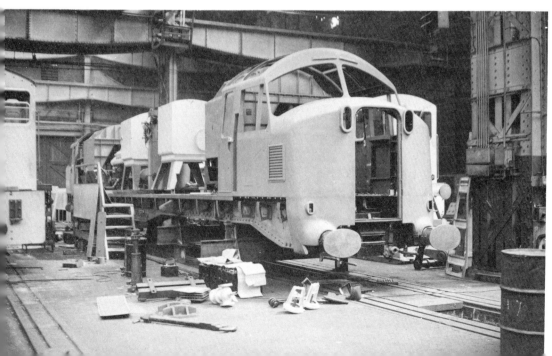

up to the 100mph they occasionally attained in the first two years.

Because of the standard vacuum brake on rolling stock and the vacuum-controlled Westinghouse air brake on the locomotive, two Westinghouse exhausters and two Westinghouse compressors driven by individual electric motors were installed. Compressors were housed in the cab noses and exhausters in the engine room. Four 10in by 8in brake cylinders on each bogie applied clasp blocks on each of the six wheels, and produced braking forces of 84 per cent of the braked weight on the driving wheels and nearly 60 per cent on the carriers.

Driving wheels were 43in diameter and carriers $39\frac{1}{2}$in. All were of the spoked type, and nothing was said in the specification about balancing to cover slight inequalities in casting. As this effect could be noticeable when the wheels were making 715rpm at top designed speed, dynamic balancing was called for about the time the first locomotive was completed, and was given at an extra cost of £16 per wheel-and-axle set. Wheel centres were cast at the foundries of Yarrow and Fairfield Shipbuilding & Engineering.

Air from compressors was used also for sanding, window wipers, and for the electro-pneumatic control system. This control had seven notches, of which the first, marked zero, was for engine idling; only on the next notch did the transmission control valves open and admit oil to the first, or starting, torque converter. Interlocks prevented reversal except when the locomotive was at standstill, and prevented any control from the unoccupied cab of the same locomotive or from the cabs of any second locomotive coupled in multiple.

No interchange of engine and transmission

Top: *Bogie frame of the D600-class A1A-A1A under erection in Glasgow*   Mitchell Library

Centre: *Double bolster for three-axle bogie of D600, showing large centre to take male element from the underframe, and manganese-steel rubbing plates for traction and braking thrusts. Imposed weight taken on corner pads*   Mitchell Library

Below: *Driving position of D600 locomotive showing brake handle to left, with main controller handle (top) and reversing lever (bottom) to right*   British Railways

makes or models was visualised by BTC or NBL, and the various pipes, connections, cables, controls and mountings were made just to suit the convenience of the moment. The multi-unit control and its jumper connections were devised solely for the coupling of two D600s or of one D600 and one or two D6300s. There was not the provision one might have expected from BTC for multi-unit coupling with one or more diesel-electrics, though for some years indiscriminate coupling of the two types had been practised in Europe. In 1962 two small orange squares were painted on each buffer beam to denote multi-unit coupling equipment; similar squares were put also on D6300–5. This was the only inter-coupling permitted with these two batches.

An interesting detail in these locomotives, applied to all subsequent WR diesel-hydraulics, was the Desilux two-tone warning horn, introduced to the GWR with the first AEC railcars of 1933–34, and made in a little shop in a side street off the Tottenham Court Road in London by a delightful Italian, C. V. Desiderio, 'discovered' by C. F. Cleaver of AEC.

Extras specified or agreed after the contract for the D600s was signed, and which led to the £1500 extra cost per locomotive, in addition to dynamic balancing of the wheel sets, included the supply of special deadman apparatus, extra tachometer equipment, cab heaters, fire detection apparatus, and the fitting of end footsteps and storage number boards, and the fitting and wiring of WR atc apparatus.

Nos D600–4 were named respectively *Active, Ark Royal, Bulldog, Conquest* and *Cossack,* and were considered as the Warship class. The first pair were the first named diesels on BR. The names were on large cast plates affixed to each side near mid length; above was a transfer of the second BR emblem. Numbers were painted on the driving cab sides and below them was the cast brass diamond works plate of NBL's Queen's Park factory. The two ends of the locomotive were not distinguished by painted letters or numbers at the beginning.

Official completion date of D600 was November 25 1957, but the locomotive was not handed over to BR until December, when brief preliminary trial runs with passenger stock were made before the locomotive left Scotland for the WR. D600 was introduced into regular service in January 1958, and D601 followed in March. Thereafter was a long gap before the others appeared from November 1958. D600–1 were the first type 4 diesels delivered to BR, antedating by three or four months the first English Electric D200 diesel-electrics.

After two or three driver training weeks, first WR activity was a demonstration trip on February 17 1958 with D600, between Paddington and Bristol with intermediate stops at Reading, Didcot and Swindon, and with a trailing load of 340 tons. Nothing spectacular in acceleration or speed was achieved on the westbound run; soon after leaving Bristol eastbound one of the engines cut out, and the last 100 miles or so back to London were run on one engine.

Gradually work was increased until on June 16 1958 for the first time the Cornish Riviera was diesel-hauled non-stop from Paddington to Plymouth, by D601. A 10-coach 375-ton load was the maximum permitted a D600 unassisted from Newton Abbot up Dainton bank (1 in 37/52) and in the opposite direction from Plymouth up to Hemerdon (1 in 42). With such a train a D600 could keep the non-stop schedule of 240min for the 225 miles on a fuel consumption of 220 to 240 gal (1800 to 2000lb), whereas the King class 4–6–0 steam locomotives consumed 8500 to 9500lb according to the weather. Diesel fuel capacity was sufficient for a round trip between London and Plymouth on one tank, even with the train heating boiler working in winter. The two fuel tanks, one above each dynastarter, were not symmetrical, one having a content of 475gal and the other 325gal.

In June 1958 brief trials were made between Plymouth and Newton Abbot with loads up to 13 coaches including the WR dynamometer car to determine the trailing loads and timings of various combinations of diesel and 4–6–0 steam locomotives, as it was foreseen that many of the summer holiday trains, even if diesel hauled, would need piloting over this section, and not enough diesels were then available for double heading. The only diesel concerned in the tests was D601, but it ran trips in conjunction with Castle class 4–6–0 No 7000 *Viscount Portal,* Hall class 4–6–0 No 4905 *Barton Hall,* and Manor class 4–6–0 No 7813 *Freshford Hall.* For the next few years combinations of WR diesel-hydraulics and steamers were a common sight on summer Saturdays over the South Devon line, with D600, D6300 and D800 diesels, and a variety of two-cylinder and four-cylinder 4–6–0s, the latter after 1960 from depots east of Newton Abbot.

Until the first dozen or so of the D800 class were in service the five D600s continued to work on the fastest Bristol and West of England trains,

*D600 about to leave Paddington in its early days
on the Torbay Express*

Peter Townend

and on their day were hard runners and good performers. On the Bristol line they could maintain mile a minute schedules with loads of 450/500 tons, and 500 tons could be hauled along the level at 68/70 mph, and at a steady 65 up the long 1 in 754/800 from Didcot to Swindon. Controlled road tests were not undertaken until December 1958, that is after the later-built D801 had undergone its tests.

Gradually the D600s were demoted after the arrival of more D800s by a reluctance of depot staffs to diagram them for the most important turns, not so much because of lack of power but because of different standards of engine performance and want of confidence in reliability. One side light was the average fuel consumption per mile over periods of 12 months and more, which was fractionally more than that of the D800s working the principal trains. Additional to passenger turns the D600s were allotted also certain braked freight duties including oil tank trains.

Despite numerous small troubles and not altogether satisfactory engine performance, D600–1 made distances in the first two years that were encouraging for an untried design in the hands of personnel that had never before driven or maintained diesels. To 27 October 1959 D600 accumulated 152,070 miles and D601 made 147,960 miles. The other three, coming into service much later, had accumulated only 48,000

to 52,000 miles by that date. Unfortunately this standard of performance was not maintained; by the end of 1964 the average annual mileages of D600–4 had fallen respectively to 70,000, 67,200, 54,250, 56,200 and 56,200, and after that time periodic mileage went down further. Part of the better performance of D600–1 may have been due to the parent-built engines and transmissions. This was also part of the reason for the long gap in delivery between D601 and D602, for NBL was just coming into production with those components.

No D603 was involved in an accident in 1960 and was sent back to NBL for repairs to both cabs, and numerous small frame, air brake and bogie details, and to have the transmission corrected. It is believed that the renewed cabs then were of sheet steel, as the light alloy maker was no longer interested in casting and fabricating odd small parts.

As time went on various minor alterations and additions were made. By the end of 1961 three spare engines for D600–4 and D6300–5 were available, but though engine changes were made from time to time none of the later build were installed. A few changes were made in auxiliaries, including removal of multiple-unit control. Double-digit roller blind train indicator panels were fitted to each end, one on each side of the end doors. All five locomotives when new were painted standard green with a white horizontal line along the underframe between cab footsteps; but not all went through the various BR painting stages, and on withdrawal D600 was standard blue, D602 was blue with yellow end panels, and D601/3/4 were standard green with yellow end panels.

All five were based at Plymouth Laira practically all their lives, but over the final few years were confined to Cornwall and only rarely worked to Exeter. In 1967 they spent a few weeks in South Wales, where they were sent to work mineral trains in place of English Electric type 3 diesel-electrics transferred to the Eastern Region. They were based at Landore, and worked out of there and Pantyffynnon; occasionally they ran as far north as Llandrindod Wells. However, in December they were returned to Laira for official withdrawal. This was the first WR step to implement the BRB policy approved in 1967 to reduce by 1974 the number of main line diesel locomotives from 2976 in 28 types to 2240 in 15 types, regard being paid to the elimination of types which had given trouble, had excessive maintenance costs, or which existed in such small numbers as to be quite non-standard. Class D600 qualified under all three headings, but in essence the policy meant the withdrawal of all diesel-hydraulics by the end of 1974.

After withdrawal all five were stored at Laira until July 1968, when D600–1 were sold for scrap to Woodham and D602–4 to Cashmore. Thus they did not come within the new BR classification scheme introduced that year. D600–1 were taken away from Laira by a Hymek, and the other three together by a Western.

Table VII—D600 Class Locomotives, WR

No	Name	Maker's works No	Date to traffic	Date of withdrawal
		Date of order 16/11/1955, Maker's Order No L76 Swindon Lot No 425		
D600	Active	27660	24/1/1958	30/12/1967
601	Ark Royal	27661	28/3/1958	30/12/1967
602	Bulldog	27662	3/11/1958	30/12/1967
603	Conquest	27663	21/11/1958	30/12/1967
604	Cossack	27664	20/1/1959	30/12/1967

CHAPTER 7

D6300 CLASS

Six secondary service B–B locomotives of power class 2 ordered from NBL at the same time as the five D600s were part of the pilot programme, but they came late. Concurrently NBL received a BTC order for 10 diesel-electric Bo–Bo locomotives of the D6100 class. These two contracts gave a clear comparison between the two forms of transmission, as they were placed at the same time with the same contractor, and both had the same engine, the same number of wheels, and generally similar bogies and bodies.

Accepted prices were £53,000 per locomotive for the diesel-hydraulics and £62,400 for the diesel-electrics. Estimated weights were around 64 tons in each case to meet a 16-ton axle load, which in the diesel-hydraulics would have warranted the yellow circle route availability on the WR. Actual all-on weights were 68 tons for the diesel-hydraulics and above 70 tons for the diesel-electrics. Various modifications specified before delivery of the batches was complete brought the diesel-hydraulic final price above £55,000 and that of the diesel-electrics to £65,000. In the general contract for the diesel-hydraulics were included a spare engine, spare transmission, and, shared with the D600, two train-heating boilers.

In November 1957, more than a year before any of the pilot six D6300–5 were delivered, a further order was placed for 52 locomotives to the same general design and specification; by the time the detail design was put in hand numerous changes were agreed in all four major aspects: engine, transmission, auxiliaries and mechanical portion. The numbers of these locomotives D6306–57, ran on from those of the pilot six, and they formed much the largest single BTC order for line service diesels placed up to that time.

Here, again, was found a parallel with diesel-electrics, for in May 1957 the BTC placed a further order with NBL for 28 more D6100s with the same engine set to 1100bhp as in D6306–57. Prices had risen, and in any case the quote for the first six diesel-hydraulics had been cut low, and the basic price for the 1100bhp version was £61,700, or eight per cent below the £66,800 for the diesel-electrics. Estimated weights were 65 and 72 tons respectively, and these estimates were much closer to the final weights than in the two pilot orders. In each case the final price was well above the tendered price, as numerous additions and modifications were made, often on instructions from the BTC, for liaison was not close, and such standard details as atc equipment had not been clarified.

By the time the second order was placed Swindon was well ahead in the construction of the first three Maybach-engined D800s, was proceeding with the next 30, and had adopted in principle the interchangeability of two engine and two transmission makes. But NBL did not tender on this basis, and quoted only as extras the variations in design from D6300–5 to make the NBL/MAN engine interchangeable with the Maybachs in the D800s (£500 per locomotive), and the NBL/Voith transmission interchangeable with the Mekydro K104 (£975 per locomotive). Nevertheless, this feature was sanctioned by the BTC at an aggregate expense above £70,000; but no Maybach engine or Mekydro drive ever ran in a D6300. Installation of a preheater was agreed at a late stage, November 1959, at a cost of another £475 per locomotive. Final prices for the 1100bhp diesel-hydraulics thus became about £64,500 for D6306–31 and about £250 more for D6332–57 which had flexible gangways and certain other details from new. Diesel-electric final price approximated to £68,200 each. Though the design of D6306–57 was largely a repeat of the first six, the drawing office charges grossed above £6000; those of D6300–6 totalled about £15,000.

Three years elapsed between the first order and the delivery of D6300 in December 1958, against the promised 18 months. Delay in delivery of the later locomotives D6306–57 also was considerable, and in this case began with the long period between receipt of the NBL tender in April 1957 and the placing of the order in November the same year. Promised delivery was to begin in February 1959 and be at the rate of three locomotives a month, which meant completion by June 1960. In the event, first delivery was four months late, and then after about 30 locomotives had been received by the WR further deliveries were suspended for five months until February 1962 to permit concentration on D833–65. Some of this delay was due to about 70 design modifications, many of which were made

NBL-built diesel-electric of D6100 class built at same time as the first group of D6300 diesel-hydraulics, and powered by the same type of diesel engine

British Railways

after immediate experience with the first few locomotives; others, such as windscreen washers, snow plough brackets, and brake accelerating devices, were asked for by the BTC, but not all modifications were applied to every locomotive.

Originally the D6300s were intended to handle all freight traffic, and secondary passenger services not handled by dmu sets, in the Devon and Cornwall No 1 conversion scheme; to act as

1000bhp diesel-hydraulic locomotive built by NBL in 1959 and set to work in January 1960

British Railways

pilots or bankers for passenger and goods trains on the steep grades between Newton Abbot and Penzance; to operate in tandem on main line trains; and to handle certain subsidiary traffic east, north and north west of Exeter convenient to units based on Newton Abbot. The 58 made up the estimated total of class 2 power needed for conversion scheme No 1, including spares and locomotives immobilised.

D6300–5 were given the NBL/MAN model L12V18/21A engine set to 1000bhp at 1445rpm; D6306–57 had the B model set to 1100bhp at 1530rpm. This latter speed was chosen so that the engines and governor settings would be the same as those going into the 30 class D800 locomotives D833–65 and the same as those of the Maybachs in the remaining D800s. For the same

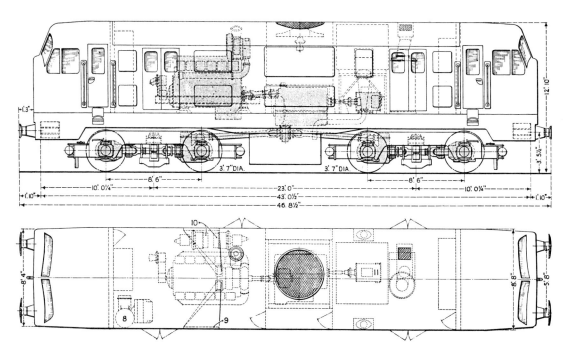

Above: Fig 9 *General layout of equipment, D6306-57*

Below: *Voith L306r transmission as used in D6300-5 showing input flange and semi-circular step-up gear casing. Output shaft and flanges at bottom*

reason the electro-pneumatic control system of D6300–5 was changed to full electric in D6306–57. Interchangeability was to be promoted also by the engine mounting sub-frame on four Metalastik feet. In D6300–5 the sub-frame rested on semi-resilient pads, and in those locomotives the engine itself was offset from the locomotive centre line, whereas in D6306–57 it was central.

Different forms of Voith transmission were installed. D6300–5 had the L306r model, made in Glasgow; D6306–57 had the LT306r, which was compact and lighter, had at the time a greater power input standardised at 1036hp with 1530 engine rpm, and had different power take-off possibilities. Heidenheim supplied 22 of these transmissions; the remainder plus spares were built by NBL. Necessary gear reductions in the drive after the hydraulic portion also were different, being 3.43:1 in D6300–5 and 4.45:1 with the LT306r.

Combination of an engine variant and a different transmission model led to the input centre line of the latter being rather higher than the crankshaft centre line in D6306–57, so the primary cardan shaft was set at an angle instead of being horizontal as in D6300–5. The step-up gears also were within the main transmission block, whereas in the first six they were in a bolted-on cast iron casing on top of the block. In the first six locomotives the transmission block rested on trunnion and sandwich mountings; in the next 52 the block was on Metalastik feet. Further, in D6300–5 the dynastarter was driven by a long cardan shaft from the back end of the step-up gears, and was mounted on a high vibration- and sound-producing welded steel carrier secured to the floor. Originally it was to be of 35kW capacity, but was altered to 50kW before the first locomotive delivery. In D6306–57 the larger dynastarter was bolted directly to the floor and driven by a short cardan from the back end of the main hydraulic shaft.

A major change in the cooling system was that the 32hp electric motor drive of the fan on the first six was replaced in D6306–57 by the Behr hydrostatic pump and motor. In each case the Serck radiator blocks were close to the centre of the locomotive length and were in a separate cooling compartment across the width of the body, which meant that all cooling air was sucked through the radiator and expelled through the roof without any subsidiary air flow through the engine room. A separate engine room ventilating fan was put into D6300–5 at an extra at a cost of £45 per locomotive. In the first six locomotives each side radiator was covered by a triple set of fixed louvres in the wall, below which was a corresponding set of ventilating louvres. In D6306–57 the radiator block was covered by a single square grille without ventilating louvres below, and the whole appearance of the side walls was cleaned up.

In the first six locomotives starting tractive effort was 45,000lb at 30 per cent adhesion and continuous rated wheel-rim effort 23,900lb at 10.4mph. The more powerful engine and revised transmission of the 52 succeeding machines gave a starting effort of 43,500lb at 30 per cent adhesion and a continuous rated effort of 30,000lb at 8mph with 1036hp input to transmission. All D6300s had a top designed speed of 75mph, but rarely, if ever, did they attain that rate, even when working in tandem with a D600 or D800, for the South Devon and Cornwall lines and services were hardly suitable for such speeds. Change-over from one converter to another took place at approximately 23 and 45mph in D6300–5 and at 26 and 50mph in D6306–57. As with the D600s the spoked wheels were 43in diameter and were dynamically balanced.

Despite the aluminium body frame, walls and cabs, the weight of D6300–5 was well above estimates. When first completed D6300 scaled 61.4 tons empty, and with the full complement of 450gal of fuel and 500gal of boiler water and all supplies the weight was 67.2 tons, due largely

to the big welded steel underframe and heavy box frames of the bogies made up of welded and rivetted steel plates and angles. When all modifications had been made and atc equipment added the empty weight was 62.3 tons and the fully laden weight 68 tons. The two bogies including wheels, axles, axle drives and brake gear accounted for 25.2 tons, the main underframe for 7.5 tons, and the superstructure for 4.5 tons. Weight summary was: mechanical portion 39.5 tons, engine equipment 11.25 tons, transmission 8.8 tons, electrical and associated equipment 2.75 tons. D6306–25 weighed 60.2 tons empty and 64.7 tons full; D6326 onwards scaled 0.3 tons more as built.

The bogies were the two-axle equivalents of the three-axle type in the D600s. The superimposed weight of around 42.5 tons total was supported on two cup-shaped flat-faced side bearers on each bogie, carried on a bolster with swing links and double full elliptic springs on each side. The first six locomotives had Timken roller

Fig 10 *Speed/tractive effort curves of the two variations of D6300 class*

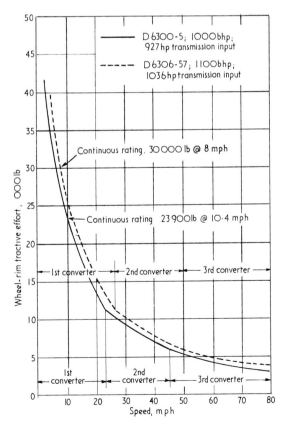

bearing axleboxes; of the next 52 locomotives D6306-31 had the Timken type and D6332-57 the SKF form. All had manganese steel thrust surfaces and were supported by compensating beams and coil springs. The pivot took no traction or braking forces.

Clasp rigging applied two blocks to each wheel through four lightweight Comprestal cylinders per bogie: 8in by 8in in the first six and 8in by 8¾in in the next 52. Respective braking forces were 45 and 50 tons, resulting from the controlled pressure in the cylinders and the different brake rigging leverage in each batch. Locomotive air brakes in the first six were Westinghouse, fed from a single Westinghouse compressor; D6306-57 had Oerlikon straight air brakes with that company's driver's valve, and in this respect were unique among WR diesel-hydraulics. For the train vacuum brakes one Westinghouse exhauster was provided in D6300-5 and two of Reavell make in D6306-57. WR atc was installed.

The fuel tank was in the roof, so feed to the engine was by gravity and the fuel injection pumps were always drowned. This tank was offset to assist a clear walkway down one side of the locomotive. A Spanner train heating boiler was put into D6300-5; a Clayton type into D6306-25, and a Vapor type into D6326-57. In later years the boiler controls were removed from those locomotives not allocated to passenger working or empty stock haulage.

Electro-pneumatic controls of D6300-5 were arranged to multiple with the D600s. To widen the multiple-unit possibilities D6306-57 were given an all-electric system to match the D800 Warships. All 52 and the relevant Warships were given painted white diamond marks on the base of the nose at each end to denote this equipment. The deadman action was by a pedal on the left-hand (driving) side and by a push button on the right-hand side.

All D6300s on coming into service were painted BR standard green, with the lion-wheel-crown emblem between the cab door and the double

side doors of the engine room on D6300-5, and inboard of the double doors on D6306-57. A horizontal light grey line ran along the underframe between the cab doors. The number appeared four times in white paint on the cab sides; below each was a diamond works plate of NBL's Queen's Park factory; and below that again was painted the WR blue circle for axle loads up to 17.6 tons. In later years most D6300s received yellow end panels or complete yellow ends, and in 1967-68 some were painted blue. Also some ran with only one works plate a side, at the centre of the solebar.

Among modifications on or after construction D6300-5 had an additional motor-driven exhauster, an engine-compartment ventilating fan, a bigger (50kW) dynastarter, and a revised deadman equipment to line up with that in D800-2; in 1960 WR atc was added and wired up. D6306-57 had atc from the beginning; their later modifications included redesign of battery boxes, extra bogie number plates, acceleration device for the air brake system, and oil separator and drainage tank. NBL put train headcode classification panels only on D6334-57 and Swindon applied them to the earlier units; NBL also put in excess temperature safeguards on D6335-57 and sent to Swindon kits of parts to suit the preceding locomotives.

Soot cleaning devices were put on D6336-57; snow plough brackets were attached to D6336-47 by NBL and possibly others were so fitted at Swindon; similar procedure was followed in the fitting of auxiliary lifting brackets to D6337-57; flexible gangways were put on by NBL from the end of 1960; footstep modifications were introduced with D6316 and ran to D6357, and were put on D6306-15 later. Nine locomotives were fitted new with window washers, but they were removed after a few months. Both D600-4 and D6300-5 suffered damaged life guards and sand pipes by running into rail stops at depots and sheds, and the shape of each was modified. The end doors and flexible gangways were for use when two D6300s were working in tandem, but only on rare occasions do these fittings seem to have been connected, and then only in Cornwall when working on passenger trains.

A few of the L12V18/21B engines from D6306-57 and D833-65 were sent to Glasgow for repair in the early 1960s, but NBL did not enthuse over such work, because the BTC expected a six-month guarantee when the engine was sent back, and to cope with this NBL almost had to turn out a new engine. This awkward requirement does not seem to have been imposed on the BR Workshops organisation at a later stage.

Before being drafted to Laira, Newton Abbot and Cornwall, new type 2 locomotives were run in from Swindon, often two in tandem to reduce track occupation, on slow passenger trains to and from Bath. At times two worked in tandem west of Plymouth on such named trains as the Cornish Riviera and Royal Duchy; but much of their service in Cornwall, on the Devon branches, and on the old SR Exeter–Barnstaple line was on light passenger and freight trains. Over the first two or three years D6300–5, apart from D6302, made quite good mileages for type 2 power. D6300 averaged 38,800 miles a year over its first three years, D6303 about 33,000 miles, and D6304 made over 40,000mpa over the same period. Fuel consumption in those early years averaged 1.45mpg. In general, the average mileage of the whole class fell as the locomotives went on to lighter duties and ecs turns.

Because of limited multiple-unit possibilities D6300–5 were confined to South Devon and Cornwall. Partly because of branch closures in those counties, and partly to the expansion of WR diesel traction by the time the last D6300 was delivered, D6306–57 spread over most of the WR system south of Birmingham, and were found at London, Reading, Bristol, Oxford, Gloucester and South Wales. They handled such subsidiary freights as Acton–High Wycombe-Princes Risborough-Banbury, and Gloucester-Forest of Dean; banked freights from Stroud up to Sapperton tunnel; and piloted Weymouth passenger trains up Evershot bank. From 1964 until withdrawal some of them handled the empty stock workings between Paddington and Old Oak Common.

The first six were the first to go, being different to the end in several details from the others, and with a more restricted range of mu coupling. D6301 was the first withdrawal, in December 1967; it was sold to Cohen but was not actually broken up for some months. The other five were withdrawn in May 1968, and all 52 of the later more powerful machines had disappeared by the end of 1971, though the official withdrawal date of D6338–9, the last two in service, was 1 January 1972.

Table VIII—D6300 Class Locomotives, WR

No	Maker's works No	Date to traffic	Date of withdrawal
Date of order 16/11/1955, Maker's Order No L77, Swindon Lot No 426			
D6300	27665	12/1/1959	26/5/1968
6301	27666	19/2/1959	30/12/1967
6302	27667	19/2/1959	26/5/1968
6303	27668	22/5/1959	26/5/1968
6304	27669	23/6/1959	26/5/1968
6305	27670	11/1/1960	26/5/1968
Date of order 5/11/1957, Maker's Order No L97, Swindon Lot No 440			
6306	27879	12/10/1959	12/12/1968
6307	27880	12/10/1959	27/3/1971
6308	27881	7/1/1960	11/9/1971
6309	27882	12/1/1960	22/5/1971
6310	27883	5/1/1960	27/3/1971
6311	27884	7/1/1960	23/9/1968
6312	27885	14/1/1960	22/5/1971
6313	27886	12/1/1960	3/8/1968
6314	27887	25/1/1960	26/4/1969
6315	27888	25/1/1960	22/5/1971
6316	27889	1/3/1960	31/3/1968
6317	27890	1/3/1960	23/9/1968
6318	27891	14/3/1960	22/5/1971
6319	27892	11/4/1960	11/9/1971
6320	27893	23/3/1960	22/5/1971
6321	27894	7/4/1960	3/8/1968
6322	27895	7/4/1960	3/10/1971
6323	27896	25/4/1960	22/5/1971
6324	27897	1/6/1960	14/9/1968
6325	27898	14/6/1960	5/10/1968
6326	27899	16/5/1960	3/10/1971
6327	27900	30/6/1960	22/5/1971
6328	27901	18/6/1960	17/7/1971
6329	27902	18/6/1960	30/11/1968
6330	27903	26/6/1960	3/10/1971
6331	27904	26/6/1960	27/3/1971
6332	27905	28/7/1960	22/5/1971
6333	27906	3/8/1960	1/1/1972
6334	27907	1/12/1960	3/10/1971
6335	27908	22/2/1961	14/9/1968
6336	27909	3/7/1961	1/1/1972
6337	27910	13/3/1962	21/10/1971
6338	27911	29/3/1962	1/1/1972
6339	27912	2/4/1962	1/1/1972
6340	27913	3/4/1962	22/5/1971
6341	27914	12/5/1962	30/11/1968
6342	27915	11/5/1962	12/12/1968
6343	27916	10/5/1962	3/10/1971
6344	27917	18/5/1962	14/9/1968
6345	27918	19/5/1962	14/9/1968
6346	27919	8/6/1962	26/4/1969
6347	27920	2/6/1962	31/3/1968
6348	27921	14/6/1962	24/7/1971
6349	27922	14/6/1962	14/9/1968
6350	27923	27/6/1962	14/9/1968
6351	27924	27/6/1962	30/11/1968
6352	27925	12/7/1962	2/5/1971
6353	27926	12/7/1962	23/9/1968
6354	27927	2/8/1962	22/5/1971
6355	27928	24/8/1962	14/9/1968
6356	27929	27/9/1962	3/10/1917
6357	27930	13/11/1962	12/12/1968

CHAPTER 8

D800 CLASS

AFTER the signing of the K-M licence agreement there was no further talk of more D600s; but the work of adapting the basic V200 design to suit WR limitations was immense. The standard BR loading gauge, and not the WR wider contour, was adopted, and while this permitted the D800s to run over most sections of the BR system it brought problems that took much solving.

The restriction put a severe test on Swindon designers, who had to adapt the V200 superstructure and bogies to a height 10in lower and a width 16in narrower than the German model and yet get in the same power plants, equipments and tank capacities. Moreover, the double-wall superstructure had glass fibre pads for sound and heat insulation accommodated within, and in the D800s they had to be reduced to 2½in thickness from 4in in the V200; the same applied to insulation on the cab bulkheads.

More than 200 detail manufacturing drawings of the V200 were sent by K-M, but dimensions throughout had to be converted from metric to English measure, and a redesign made to get the narrower and lower superstructure while maintraining strength; checks were made at all stages of the stress calculations throughout the whole of the new body framing. Much time was consumed by sheer translation from German to English. In the end, something like 75,000 manhours of drawing office time were absorbed in adjusting the whole locomotive design to British limitations, preparing new calculations and shop drawings, and summarising material requirements. This work, and the concomitant building techniques that had to be evolved in the factory, resulted in a time of 2¼ years from the receipt of the last K-M drawings in February 1956 to the completion of the first locomotive in June 1958.

About this time both the DB and Maybach were making certain changes and improvements to be incorporated in 50 new V200 locomotives, but to hasten delivery of material coming from Germany and to ensure the new builder, the BTC, did not have to put in anything untried, the components installed were the standards used elsewhere up to 1956. This resulted in the first three Swindon locomotives, D800–2, differing in certain details and power output from the succeeding 68 D800 class locomotives.

First of the Swindon built D800s at the head of an express, in its original condition of 1958 with old type of train headcode indicator frame

45

In seeking the combined lightness and strength needed for 2000bhp on four axles and under 80 tons all-on weight, stressed-skin techniques evolved gradually in aviation and structural steel industries were employed. Here the thin plates of the body sides and roof were stress-bearing and contributed to the strength. There was no separate underframe of large standard-section steel joists and angles.

The superstructure supported all equipment except the two bogies, but on a full crane lift had to carry their weight. It had to absorb drag forces, and end buffing loads up to 200 tons; withstand lifting strains with all equipment in position, from either a lift or a jacking at one end or the other, or a lift with slings or jacks near both ends; and possibly, in derailments, had to be lifted by jacks applied to the sides. In untoward end collisions, it was permitted to suffer only partial or gradual collapse, so that much of the collision shock would be absorbed by local deformation. For economic reasons, and to facilitate repair of local damage, such a structure had to be fabricated of ordinary mild steel.

Above: Driving position of D800-2 showing in foreground handle of the six power-notch control. To the left is socket for the continuous-brake handle; forward of it is the Knorr straight air brake handle

British Railways

Below: Stressed-skin superstructure of a D800 under fabrication at Swindon

British Railways

Main members in the lower part were two $6\frac{1}{2}$in od steel tubes 5mm(0.197in) thick that ran from end to end. Ideally they should have run direct from buffer to buffer to take end loads with least tendency to buckle, but the British loading gauge and buffer height, combined with the necessary location and dimensions of engines, transmission blocks, bogies and other items made this impracticable in the D800s. In practice the buffers were a few inches below the tube line and additional platework had to be

welded in to bring the buffing loads gradually up to the tubes. In one or two collisions the tubes were bent, but it was possible to straighten them and even weld in new sections. The main tubes ran through a number of cross stretchers of 4mm (0.157in) steel plate, which were themselves welded also to 4mm(0.157in) plate longitudinals outside of and between the tubes. All were welded into one honeycomb assembly supplemented by a 4mm(0.157in) deck plate, and at the ends by drag boxes and buffer beams. Within this frame were carried the separate welded-up fuel tanks.

Welded to this structure were the body side frame members of 12swg(0.104in) folded steel angle, Z and other sections, and the 14swg(0.08 in) side sheets which went up beyond the strong double cantrails and curved in to form the non-removable stress-bearing part of the roof. Thus from the body bolsters above the trucks to the top of the roof, and from end to end, was a single fully welded structure of which every part took some share in the loading. To maintain strength of the walls, only two windows were put in each side, but comprehensive internal lighting gave ample visibility. The bulbous noses of the German V200 could not just be copied because of the restrictions of the loading gauge and a slight redistribution of minor equipment, and a squatter contour had to be styled.

This complete steel structure weighed only 11.13 tons for its 58ft length, 8ft 9in width and 11ft maximum depth. The only light alloy parts were the five removable hatches in the roof and the internal doors, the weights of which are not included in the total just given. These detachable sections covered practically the whole roof area between the cab bulkheads, and enabled complete engines and transmission blocks to be lowered in and lifted out.

The frame was a fine example of modern design to which no exception could be raised. Not so the K-M bogie, which was the controversial point in the whole locomotive, and did not give satisfactory riding at high speed until much study and important modifications had been made, as detailed in chapter 13. Lack of easy lateral movement was the trouble. Though this was a deliberate part of the design it had arisen at first only as a secondary factor, for the real origin of the bogie had been to get a design into which the transmission output gears would drop and in which no wear could take place at any point.

Different track conditions in the two countries have been advanced as a reason for the troubles in England not found in Germany; but speed

Table IX—Constituent weights of D803-12; tons

Frame and superstructure	11.13	
Fuel tanks	1.20	
Water tanks	1.16	
	13.49	13.49
Pipes, conduits and fittings		7.83
2 bogies, including wheels and axles		16.70
2 Maybach engines	9.10	
2 cooling groups	4.00	
2 preheaters	0.23	
2 engine bedframes	0.50	
	13.83	13.83
2 transmissions plus cardans and 4 axle drives		7.10
Battery	1.8	
Elect. equip. including dynastarter	4.5	
2 exhausters and 1 compressor	1.8	
Train heating boiler and controls	1.7	
Fire fighting equipment	0.25	
	10.05	10.05
Total empty weight		69.00
Contained water and oil in engines and transmissions, etc.		1.40
Fuel		3.10
Water		4.50
Sand and man		0.60
Weight with full supplies		78.60

seems to have been the only factor. Because of track, signalling and other limitations in post-war Western Germany, top speed there throughout the 1950s was limited to 75mph(120kmph), and the subsequent increases came almost entirely through improved conditions following electrification, and so were not within the orbit of the V200s. Above 80mph the bogie proved unsatisfactory on the WR, and was felt to be almost dangerous in those first happy few months of the D800s when drivers ran up to 95/100mph. In Germany good running was maintained up to 75mph; no bogie there ever had to be altered, and they continue to run with satisfaction to this day.

The K-M bogie had no physical pivot and no separate sprung bolster. Superstructure weight was taken through pins on the buckles of large inverted plate springs on each side of the truck, and was transmitted through swing links and coil springs to the bogie frame. Superimposed weight on each bogie was about 17 tons a side. Each

Completely welded frame for K-M type of bogie used in D800 locomotives

British Railways

Axlebox arms with supporting rubber-bushed trunnions at near end; in the centre is the axle drive casing and torque reaction arm with rubber bushing at near end British Railways

axlebox had a further overhung plate spring of its own. These boxes were not of normal type with flat guides; to maintain the 'wear-less' principle each roller bearing was in a housing that formed a thrust arm connected to the centre transom of the bogie frame through a large pin and bonded rubber bushing.

As there was no centre pivot the turning action was about a 'virtual centre', obtained by four bell-cranks connected by cross and longitudinal links, which provided also for a small amount of side movement by the deflection of the rubber bushes surrounding the eight pins of the link movement, supplemented by the deflection of the rubber in the pivots of the axlebox arms. The longitudinal links were connected at one end to the bogie-mounted bell-cranks and at the other end to brackets secured to the locomotive super-structure. Traction and braking thrusts between body and bogie were taken through curved manganese steel pads set to a gap of 2mm when stationary.

Unsprung weight per axle with $39\frac{1}{2}$in diameter wheels and Maybach C33 axle drive was 2.55 tons. Separate tyres were shrunk on to the discs, and were braked through two shoes per wheel by Knorr-type straight air brakes, applied by a vacuum-controlled proportional system that applied the vacuum brakes down the train at the same time, or permitted straight air braking of the locomotive alone. Braking force in D800–2 came from eight Laycock-Knorr short-stroke 8in by $5\frac{5}{8}$in cylinders which gave a braking force of 54.8 tons with 45 lb/sq in pressure in the cylinders. As in standard European practice a pas-

senger/goods valve was fitted to retard the normal application when operating fitted or partly fitted freights to prevent bunching of the wagons. At the time of D800 construction no air braked freights ran on the WR.

The air brake system was linked to the dead-man pedal with an action delay of 5sec before the oil engines were brought to idling, followed by a light and then a stronger brake application to prevent bunching. Engines could be started and idled at any time, but electric interlocks ensured that the transmission could not be brought in and load taken up unless there was sufficient air and vacuum in the braking systems. Any brake failure in running also brought the engines back to idling.

While D800–2 were under construction objection was raised to the small wheel diameter in relation to load carried. This vertical loading was known as the P/D ratio, P being the axle load in tons and D being the tread diameter in feet. The question arose through the reading in England of a University of Illinois report on stresses in rolling cylinders, and as a result the civil engineer laid down a ratio of 5, whereas the ratio of D800–2 was 6. The limit imposed by BR civil engineers with no experience of diesels running over their rails took no account of the reasons for troubles with the wheels of American diesels and with the rails over which they ran. In the USA frequent high braking loads and wheel slides led to shelling and spalling of the tyres, flats on the wheels, and burnt rail heads. Many railways abroad had trouble-free wheel loadings of 600 to 700lb/in diameter; D800 had 563lb against the 575lb of the heaviest V200. In

Right: *Revised Mekydro K104 as installed in D803-32 with cast iron converter casing block supported at three points on cylindrical trunnions. Double output flanges at bottom*

Right: *Revised Mekydro K104 as installed in D803-32 with cast iron converter casing block supported at three points on cylindrical trunnions. Double output flanges at bottom*

view of the lack of trouble with these examples the WR management insisted that the design should be kept to the $39\frac{1}{2}$in wheel, and this gave no trouble in the years of operation of 71 locomotives.

Within the superstructure the two sets of power-transmission equipment with individual cooler groups were located symmetrically about the locomotive centre, as shown in Fig. 11. The dynastarter was in the end nose, and the cardan shaft driving it ran below the floor of the driving cab, which was more than 6ft above rail level. In the V200 a clear passage down each side gave non-stoop walking; the reduced BR loading gauge resulted in a cramped passage that involved a cross-over from one side to the other.

Equipment layout ensured that the output gears of the transmission were on the bogie centre lines, and only short and equal cardan shafts were needed to reach the spiral bevel axle drives, which lay within cast steel casings and had pump lubrication. The reaction torque arms had rubber-bushed pivot pins on the same line as the axle-box arms. Swindon obtained these drives dismantled, pressed the main gear on the axle and then assembled the other wheel and the casing.

On entering regular service D800 went briefly on to the Bristol route and then to the Plymouth services, including the non-stop Cornish Riviera with the maximum 10-coach load permitted without a pilot west of Newton Abbot. At once it began to build up a mileage of 380 to 400 a day, though for some months it worked on steam turns and not on diagrams drawn up specially for

Fig 11 *Layout of equipment, D800 class. Key:*
1—Diesel engine
2—Hydraulic transmission
3—Axle drives
4—Cooler group
5—Train heating boiler
6—Fuel tanks

diesels. Its performances, and those of D801-2 from the end of 1958, seemed to justify the choice of the V200 as a good basic model; but the first practical application of the decision to make the D800 the standard WR type 4 machine —the order on Swindon in February 1957 for another 30—led to some detail changes from the three prototypes.

For these 30 Swindon-built locomotives, Nos D803-32, Maybach supplied all 60 engines plus three spares, but to initiate the new Maybach licensee, BSE, 10 of these engines were knocked down and sent in parts to the Ansty works for BSE to reassemble. In a sense the three spares became five, for after the order was placed a decision was made to put another make of engine into D830. Similar procedure applied to the Mekydros, Maybach supplying 60 sets plus five spares, while Stone re-erected three from dismantled parts. Cardan shafts in D800-2 were of Maybach make; in D803-32 and D866-70 they were of Gelenkwellenbau (GWB) make. D833-65

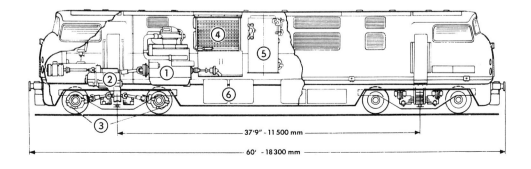

37'9" - 11 500 mm
60' - 18 300 mm

had Glasgow-built NBL/MAN engines, NBL/ Voith transmissions, and GWB cardan shafts supplied through Hardy-Spicer. Twenty transmissions were built at Heidenheim and the rest at Glasgow. All 120 axle drives for D803–32 came from Maybach, and the 152 for D833–70 were of Maybach design from Stone. The two Paxman Ventura engines put into D830 were coupled to Mckydro transmissions.

Changes from D800–2 found in D803–32 included a redesigned torque converter to give greater input capacity, and the use of a seven power-notch control in place of six power notches. From 1950 to 1956 the Mekydro permanently-filled converter was in a water-jacketed integrally-cast aluminium alloy casing, and had a maximum input capacity around 960/970hp, which did not match up to the 1200 metric bhp UIC rating of the MD650 engine. Also, leaks between oil and water passages occurred from time to time because of the differential expansion of two metals under oil temperature changes, for the aluminium housing was bolted to a cast iron gear case.

From 1957 the converter casing was of cast iron with external ribs, and the transmission oil was circulated continuously through a water-cooled heat exchanger attached to the main transmission block. This change was made as soon as a design was evolved in which the new converter assembly could be made interchangeable with the old; it enabled the transmission input to be increased from 966hp at 1400rpm(engine speed) in D800–2 to 1035hp at 1530rpm(engine speed) in D803–32 and D866–70. With the new converter the support of the whole main transmission block was changed from three rigid spherical trunnion mountings to three elastically supported cylindrical trunnions, but this change was not initiated until D813.

Some power loss at idling while running was experienced with the Mekydros because the converter was always full. Consideration was given to an arrangement by which separate action on the part of the driver would empty the converter temporarily if the engine was to idle for any length of time. One mechanism to do this was obtained, but was never fitted, for the idea had been to apply it to a locomotive equipped for electric train heating, a proposal that did not come to fruition.

Operation of D800–2 soon showed the six power notches of the control to be insufficient for smooth acceleration and economy. The lowest, or zero, notch was for engine idling only, at

Table X—Notches and speeds of D800 Class Control

1	2	3	4	5	6	7
		D800-2		D803-32		D833-65
		Initial rpm	Revised rpm	Initial rpm	Revised rpm	Initial rpm
0	Idling	600	620	600	620	600
1	Power	600	620	600	620	600
2	,,	900	950	1000	950	950
3	,,	1050	1140	1100	1140	1140
4	,,	1200	1275	1200	1275	1275
5	,,	1300	1370	1300	1370	1370
6	,,	1400	1440	1400	1460	1460
7	,,	—		1530	1530	1530

600rpm; then the six power notches gave in succession the speeds shown in column 3 of Table X. Power-plant control in D800–2 was an all-electric Brown Boveri (BBC) system. All three equipments were supplied by the BBC works at Mannheim, Germany; BBC personnel actually wired up D800 throughout and provided instruction to Swindon electricians, who did the work on all succeeding Swindon-built diesel-hydraulics. All wires were run in galvanised conduit; four, and later six, spare wires ran from end to end down the main conduit for use in service should a fault develop and to cover any modifications that might be made, this being much easier than trying to pull extra wires through a full conduit in a completed locomotive.

The BBC all-electric system, incorporating multiple-unit control of two locomotives with four engine-transmission plants, and including warning and protective devices, lighting and auxiliary circuits, involved in D803 onwards 36-contact jumper connections, of which 30 pairs of contacts were in use with multi-coupling, and the others spare. About 2½ miles of small cable lay within a D800 locomotive.

To overcome the difficulties of the widely-spaced notches, the BBC control in D803 *et seq* was provided with one idling and seven power notches after proposals by Maybach to have eight power notches, but there was still the slight difference at first in that D803–12 could be multi-coupled only among themselves; the others could be coupled up also to D6306–57. With only six power notches D800–2 could be coupled in multiple only among themselves. Seven power notches was the maximum practicable without major alterations to the whole control scheme, and that was undesirable, as construction of D803 and its followers was well ahead by the time the operational results of D800–2 were digested.

Under the new control scheme, and with the reinforced torque converter, the Maybach engines

Above: *NBL-built D840* Resistance *on test train before leaving Scotland for Swindon. Later type of kicking plate below cab door; fan holes in roof reinforced. Near buffer shows NBL order number*

Right: *Front end of one of the last Swindon-built batch of D800s, near the end of its life after being painted blue and given the last BR emblem in 1968. Collision damage in cab plates surrounding side access doors*

British Railways

Below: *Highest numbered D800 was D870, here seen on a Cardiff—Manchester train near Church Stretton on the West-to-North line. Warning horns above cab roof*

Derek Cross

were set to 1135bhp at 1530rpm. The NBL/
MAN engines in D833–65 were set to 1100bhp
at the same revs. The Paxman engines in D830
were also set to 1135bhp at 1530rpm. Only
D800–2 retained their original top speed of
1400rpm.

Original settings of the Maybach engines in
D803 onwards were as given in column 5 of
Table X. At a later stage they were altered to
keep furthur away from criticals near idling speed
and to provide a more even spread of power
between the notches, and by 1962 were as shown
in column 6. NBL/MAN settings from new were
as given in column 7. About the same time and
for the same reasons the settings of D800–2 were
altered to the values shown in column 4. The set
engine output at these different rotational speeds
was not in direct ratio to the revs.

In the mid 1960s the multiple-unit coupling
section of the control was removed from many
D800s, because it was never used yet was liable
to earthing and faults due to ingress of damp. In
1968 it had to be re-installed in a number of
locomotives when the practice of working two
D800s in tandem was regularised for certain
accelerated express passenger trains. All the locomotives re-equipped were Maybach-Mekydros
and included D819/22/3/4/7/8/9/31/2/66/7/
8/9. These then had the two white diamonds
re-painted on the nose base between the buffers.

Main change in the Maybach engine through
the D800 class was in the mounting. The three-
point ball-trunnion support of the engine-carry-
ing frame in D800–2 was perpetuated in D803–
12 except for D809. The last-numbered locomotive, plus D813–29, D831–32, and D866–70
had four Metalastik resilient feet of Cushymount
type, and the closed-ring carrying frame as a
whole, plus its mountings, was interchangeable
between MAN and Maybach engines, though
the actual bolting of the engine to the carrying
frame was different in the two makes. The
Paxman engines in D830 were longer and could
not be accommodated on the standard frame.

Maybach engines in D800–2 had pistons with
cast iron bodies below the heat resisting detachable steel crown; in succeeding D800s with the
same make of engine this body was replaced by
one of forged aluminium alloy. In time the
engines of D800–2 received the aluminium alloy
body, but the engine output remained at 1035bhp
because these three locomotives ran to the end
with the original lower input transmissions.

In D800–2 the safety controls shut down the
engines automatically if water temperature at the

*Three-point flexible mounting of engine-subframe
group in D800-2. The remainder of the class had a
similar subframe with four point resilient mounting*
British Railways Board

cooler entry exceeded about 90°C. This was
due to a misunderstanding, but it was perpetuated
to D832. Then a different automatic safety relay
was adopted to bring back the engine only to
idling; this was used from new in certain NBL-
built D800s and in D866–70, and later was
inserted in the older locomotives. Thermostats in
the engine control system of D800–2 were set
so that no start was possible if the cooling water
temperature was below 40°C; when the cooling
water radiator entry temperature reached 76°C
the shutters in the side walls began to open and
the fan speed to increase; temperature fluctuated
only to 2° or 3°C above and below the normal
figure of 82°C, and if temperature rose to 91°C
the automatic cut to idling came into operation.

In D800–2 the control of the two 16.5kW
dynastarters when acting as generators gave a
voltage variation from 135 at no load down to
120 at full load; from D803 onwards the control
was altered to give a tension almost constant at
110V, and the engine control, lighting and
auxiliary supplies were at that figure. The 56-cell
276a-h DP battery in D800–2 was replaced in
all other D800s by a 48-cell battery of the same
make and discharge capacity.

Mekydro transmissions installed in D800–2
had a step-up gear ratio of 2:1 which gave
2800rpm to the converter shaft. Gear change-
over points were at 24, 40 and 67mph when
working at full engine speed on the top power
notch; on lower notches the change-over speeds
were lower. These values were maintained in the
later Swindon-built D800s.

Fig. 12 shows the wheel-rim efforts of D800–2,
D803–29 and D833–65. Continuous rated tractive efforts of the two Maybach-Mekydro

batches were high at 43,800lb and 45,000lb at 11.8mph respectively. The carefully conducted controlled road tests with D801 and the ensuing check calculations confirmed these curves closely, and suggested that anything on the up-speed curve from an effort of 40,000lb at 12mph could be taken as a continuous rating. At different locations the dynamometer car recorded drawbar pulls of 35,500lb at 10.5mph, 15,400lb at 30mph, 9000lb at 50mph, 6000lb at 70mph, and 4050lb at 95mph.

At times 48,000lb was reached by D801 in the controlled road tests using the top power notch at 7 to 8mph without slip, and this meant an adhesion factor of 3.64, or 27.5 per cent adhesion. Efficiency right through the transmission from engine to axle peaked 82.5 per cent in each gear stage; and as the fourth gear stage was proportioned for a top possible speed of something like 120mph the efficiency was still high at 100mph, and presumably helped the attainment of that speed down gradients as flat as 1 in 750/850 with 250 tons trailing.

The Voith LT306r transmission in D833–65 had to cover the 0–90mph track speed range in three stages as against the four of Mekydro, but was ordered as a duplicate of those in D6306–57

Fig 12 *Speed/tractive effort curves of three variations of D800 class*

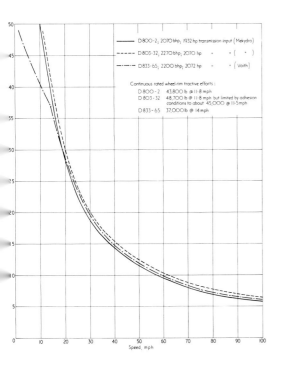

which locomotives had a speed range of 0–75 mph. As the standard D800 axle drives had to be used and the bogie wheel diameter was different from that of the D6300s there was little opportunity of getting the high potential performance over the whole of the increased speed range. The top speed converter in D833–65 did not come into operation until 65/66mph; and though it had a high efficiency from that point up to 100 mph some sacrifice had to be made at the low speed end, and the continuous rated tractive effort was 37,000lb at 14mph. Some later spare LT306r transmissions had a different gear ratio within the transmission block, so that changeover speeds from one converter to another were more favourable.

The order for the 33 NBL locomotives was dated 3 July 1958 against the maker's offer of 10 January 1958, but only a slight part of the delay arose because of need to supplement the NBL licence arrangements with K-M. The contract was on a cost-plus basis with a maximum basic price of £111,000 per locomotive; with agreed extras of a Stone-Vapor train heating boiler at £1267 and full-electric BBC control with seven power notches at £2900 per locomotive the maximum accepted price went up to £115,167. The amount allowed for profit was the amount by which the actual cost fell short of the basic £111,000, or £8500 per locomotive, whichever was the less. The K-M licence fees were adjusted between the two parties, but NBL reimbursed the BTC £200/locomotive for the proportion of technical aid provided by Swindon. Should the ascertained cost plus £8500 be less than £111,000 then the difference was to be divided equally between the BTC and NBL. In the event NBL made no profit out of the contract, quite apart from any application of the late-delivery penalty clause.

A full set of D803–32 drawings was sent from Swindon to NBL for the construction of D833–65, and any necessary alterations to suit the NBL/MAN engines and NBL/Voith transmissions were done in Glasgow. The modifications were supplemented before the first delivery by the supply of extras on the quote of Laycock-Knorr air brake equipment for the locomotive. During the period of delivery other sanctioned modifications were carried out, for the NBL tender had not taken account of various fittings in D803–32 that the WR desired to perpetuate. Excess temperature relays, and a further relay to bring the engines to idling instead of shut-down, were put new on D852–65, and NBL

One of the last NBL-built D800s, showing boiler
room air-intake and ventilating louvres cut in the
curve of the cab roof on one side only, above the
nameplate   B. Webb

supplied kits of parts to enable Swindon to so
modify D833–51. Zwicky automatic fuel-filling
shut-off valves were put as an extra on D856–65
when new, and the previous 23 locomotives were
so equipped gradually at Swindon, as were D803–
32 and D866–70. A curious point in all the
Glasgow-built locomotives was the 198mm(7.8in)
axlebox journal diameter; all other D800s had
180mm(7.1in) journals.

Except for small details the L12V18/21B
engines in D833–65 were the same as those built
for the single-engined D6306–57, but those small
details were sufficient to prevent the engines being
strictly interchangeable. The engines were kept
to the locomotive class for which they had been
ordered and of the five spare engines ready by
the end of 1961 to cover the two locomotive
classes, four had to be adjusted to suit the D800s
and one to suit the D6306 class, for which there
were already one or two spares.

Though nominally of the same capacity as
the engines in D6306–57, the cooling requirements in D833–65 were slightly different because
of small modifications in thermostat settings and
pump circulation.

Though Maybach, BSE/Maybach and NBL/
MAN engines were interchangeable as to mountings and connections, the Mekydro K104U and
Voith LT306r transmission blocks were not, and
the differences between the two meant the cardan
shaft layouts were not quite the same, and the
shafts themselves were not interchangeable. In
the Maybach/ Mekydro D800s the primary driving cardan sloped downwards from engine to
transmission; in the MAN/Voith combinations it
sloped upwards at 3° 15′. In the former the
dynastarter cardan was horizontal; in the latter

it was angled upwards to the dynastarter at 9°
47′. The transmission output flanges were in the
same location, and the cardans to the axle drives
had a downward inclination at 5° 11′ to reach
axle centre line. Thus full interchangeability of
engines and transmissions was not achieved.

Small differences in superstructure fittings,
particularly at the ends, were noticeable in the
various D800 batches. D800–2 began life with
large three-digit GW pattern train number panel
frames supplemented by lamps and folding discs
to show the still current train classification head-
lamp code and were perpetuated in D803–12.
Then to suit the new BR train description code
D813 *et seq* had the four-digit illuminated roller
blind indicator composed of two hinged and
locked two-digit frames, one on each side of the
nose centre line, with switches on the driving
dashboard to illuminate them. Double access
doors on each side of the cab appeared new in
D813 and were featured in all subsequent construction and later put on D800–12.

Deterioration of the side panels below the cab
doors was soon noticeable on D800–2, and before
long Swindon was trying 17in square serrated
green rubber kicking plates; but they soon
decayed and eventually metal kicking plates with
vertical ribs were fitted. Inset handles for operating fire extinguishers from outside were put in
adjacent to the bottoms of the cab doors, one
at each side arranged diagonally. No end footsteps were fitted to the first 13 Swindon-built
D800s when new; they came with D813 from
Swindon and D833 from NBL and were attached
to the buffer sockets (top) and cab nose (bottom).
Later they were put on D800–12 and appeared
new on D866–70.

All D800s were built new with WR electro-mechanical atc apparatus but in 1968 dual BR/WR electro-magnetic automatic warning system equipment was installed in D803–21, and the new brake application valve (vacuum), change-end switch, vacuum horn, bell, electro-pneumatic valve and timing reservoir were put on the cab bulkhead behind the driver, along with terminal boxes and conduit to the change-end switch and ep valve. D821 in the early 1960s was given a special deadman and aws application operated by compressed air instead of vacuum and had no emergency automatic brake valve. It remained the only example. Consideration was given in 1968 to the fitting of continuous air brake equipment to cater for air-braked passenger trains, but no satisfactory arrangement could be evolved largely owing to space requirements, and the D800s were thus never fitted.

The class generally were fitted with independent control of exhausters when working in multiple, so that any exhauster could be switched on from the cab in use, even if a defect had developed in the adjacent engine. D870 was unique in the location of the Desilux warning horns above the cab roof, instead of the standard mounting below the buffer beam. Over the fan openings in the roof of all locomotives were longitudinal angles with cross bars to give a walkway along the roof, and in D866–70 the fan holes were stiffened with a low rim.

Train heating boilers in D800–2 were Spanner mark Ia type of the 2000lb/hr evaporation prescribed for all type 4 diesels. D803–12 also had the Spanner mark Ia, but D813–65, except D818, had the Stone-Vapor make. D818 was odd man out, with a Spanner mark IIIa. D866–70 had the Spanner mark Ia. Boiler room ventilation and air intake grilles were cut in the roof curve from D833 onwards when new, and in most, if not all, of the others later. The grilles were on one side only.

In the early 1960s consideration was given to up-rating the Maybach MD650 engine so that it could also drive a train-heating electric generator. This could have been done by charge-air cooling. Firm proposals were made to instal the equipment in D870; some components were ordered, and jumper connections put on the locomotive but nothing further was done.

Maybach/Mekydro D800s were close to 70 tons empty and 78.6 tons full with all supplies and in working order. NBL locomotives exceeded 72 tons empty, and their all-on weight was above 80 tons. No D830, the most powerful of all on the BS rating of the engines, was also the lightest, for the Paxman engines were not quite so heavy as the other two makes, and the locomotive empty weight was around 69.5 tons, and 78 tons all-on. All D800s had tank capacities of 800gal fuel for engine and boiler, and 940gal boiler water.

D800 began to run in June 1958, and on July 14 of that year was named *Sir Brian Robertson* at a ceremony at Paddington. Otherwise the locomotives were given warship names, and were known as the Warship class despite the dissimilarity with D600–4, which also bore warship names. D812 was originally allocated the name *Despatch*, which it never carried; it was formally named *The Royal Naval Reserve 1859–1959* at Paddington on 13/11/1959 and the same evening worked The Mayflower to Plymouth. The *Despatch* nameplates lay in the stores for years. Two other allocated names were altered because of protracted delivery from NBL, and details are given at the foot of Table XI.

When built, all D800s had the whole body, louvres, fixed part of the roof and the noses painted BR standard locomotive green; the applied horizontal waist line between the two cabs, and the numerals, were in light grey; the seven removable roof panels were mid grey; tyre sides and wheel hubs were bright polished; buffer stocks and drawhook protector were red; and the drawhook, buffer step, stirrup, bogie frames and other details were black. Below the numerals was the WR $4\frac{1}{2}$in red circle denoting more than 17.6 tons axle-load route classification.

On the side walls between the two sets of radiator louvres was the cast aluminium name plate; except for D812 this bore the words 'Warship Class' below the name. Above the nameplate was the second version of the BR lion and wheel device in transfer, with the lion rising from the crown facing left. D800–2 had the nameplate 2in higher than the others. The two ends of the locomotive were denoted A and B; this was prescribed from the beginning, but not all early locomotives had the letters painted on, below the cab doors, when new.

From around the end of 1964 most D800s re-appearing from Swindon after an overhaul were painted maroon; more than half the class was so treated. From 1967 the standard colour for re-painting was blue, but in the first repaint, D865, maroon was retained for the side skirts. Later, blue engines were given either yellow end panels or full yellow ends, and yellow ends were also applied to some locomotives still in maroon. From around 1965 depot codes were stencilled once on each side at diagonal corners; from 1967 depot numbers often appeared at all four corners. In 1962 the two white diamond coupling code was first put on the nose bases to each side of the drawhook to denote multiple-unit coupling equipment, but were taken off if multiple-unit apparatus was removed.

As a result of BR 1967 policy to reduce substantially the number of diesel locomotive types, withdrawals of D800s began in August 1968 with D801, and the first three were withdrawn before any others; they stood for many months at Newton Abbot before going to Swindon for dismantling. D800 had an accumulated mileage above one million. The last of the class was withdrawn at the end of 1972. Outside Swindon works office still (April 1974) stands the shell of D818, a rusting exhibit to visitors of what a

Warship looked like. Another of the class is used by the Research Department of BRB as a test unit to provide power at Derby and D821 in a more or less serviceable condition is in private ownership.

The D800s were expensive! D800–2 cost £143,000 apiece with all drawing office time and tooling charges marked against the three. The next 30, D803–32, without any office or jig charges cost £119,000 each, and the final D866–70 were marked at £122,313—a high shop cost when engine-transmission-control price was eight per cent less than a single slow-speed engine and electric transmission of the same output. With drawing office and tooling charges already absorbed by previous orders, the last 31 DB class V200 locomotives in 1958–59 cost under DM1 million, which at the then DM11.2 to the £ exchange rate was £88,000 each.

Table XI—D800 Class Locomotives, WR

No	Name	Maker's works no	Date to traffic	Date of withdrawal
Date of order 1/1956, Built at Swindon, Lot No 428				
D800	Sir Brian Robertson	—	11/8/1958	5/10/1968
801	Vanguard	—	7/11/1958	3/8/1968
802	Formidable	—	16/12/1958	5/10/1968
Date of order 2/1957, Built at Swindon, Lot No 437				
803	Albion	—	16/3/1959	1/1/1972
804	Avenger	—	23/4/1959	3/10/1971
805	Benbow	—	13/5/1959	24/10/1972
806	Cambrian	—	3/6/1959	2/11/1972
807	Caradoc	—	24/6/1959	26/9/1972
808	Centaur	—	8/7/1959	3/10/1971
809	Champion	—	19/8/1959	3/10/1971
810	Cockade	—	16/9/1959	3/12/1972
811	Daring	—	14/10/1959	1/1/1972
812	The Royal Naval Reserve 1859-1959	—	12/11/1959	3/11/1972
813	Diadem	—	9/12/1959	1/1/1972
814	Dragon	—	1/1/1960	7/11/1972
815	Druid	—	20/1/1960	3/10/1971
816	Eclipse	—	17/2/1960	1/1/1972
817	Foxhound	—	9/3/1960	3/10/1971
818	Glory	—	30/3/1960	1/11/1972
819	Goliath	—	25/4/1960	3/10/1971
820	Grenville	—	4/5/1960	2/11/1972
821	Greyhound	—	25/5/1960	3/12/1972
822	Hercules	—	15/6/1960	3/10/1971
823	Hermes	—	6/7/1960	3/10/1971
824	Highflyer	—	27/7/1960	3/12/1972
825	Intrepid	—	24/8/1960	23/8/1972
826	Jupiter	—	7/9/1960	18/10/1971
827	Kelly	—	4/10/1960	1/1/1972
828	Magnificent	—	19/10/1960	28/5/1971
829	Magpie	—	23/11/1960	26/8/1972
830	Majestic	—	19/1/1961	26/3/1969
831	Monarch	—	11/1/1961	3/10/1971
832	Onslaught	—	8/2/1961	16/12/1972

[1] Name Zealous originally allotted, but never carried
[2] Name Zenith originally allotted, but never carried

No	Name	Maker's works no	Date to traffic	Date of withdrawal
Date of order 3/7/1958, Built by NBL, Maker's Order No L100, Swindon Lot No 443				
833	Panther	27962	6/7/1960	3/10/1971
834	Pathfinder	27963	26/7/1960	3/10/1971
835	Pegasus	27964	5/8/1960	3/10/1971
836	Powerful	27965	13/9/1960	22/5/1971
837	Ramillies	27966	8/11/1960	22/5/1971
838	Rapid	27967	3/10/1960	27/3/1971
839	Relentless	27968	12/11/1960	3/10/1971
840	Resistance	27969	3/2/1961	26/4/1969
841	Roebuck	27970	14/12/1960	3/10/1971
842	Royal Oak	27971	20/12/1960	3/10/1971
843	Sharpshooter	27972	2/1/1961	22/5/1971
844	Spartan	27973	16/3/1961	3/10/1971
845	Sprightly	27974	7/4/1961	3/10/1971
846	Standfast	27975	12/4/1961	22/5/1971
847	Strongbow	27976	22/4/1961	27/3/1971
848	Sultan	27977	27/4/1961	26/3/1969
849	Superb	27978	29/5/1961	22/5/1971
850	Swift	27979	8/6/1961	22/5/1971
851	Temeraire	27980	10/7/1961	22/5/1971
852	Tenacious	27981	24/7/1961	3/10/1971
853	Thruster	27982	30/8/1961	3/10/1971
854	Tiger	27983	26/9/1961	3/10/1971
855	Triumph	27984	25/10/1961	3/10/1971
856	Trojan	27985	16/11/1961	22/5/1971
857	Undaunted	27986	11/12/1961	3/10/1971
858	Valorous	27987	15/12/1961	3/10/1971
859	Vanquisher	27988	9/1/1962	27/3/1971
860	Victorious	27989	22/1/1962	27/3/1971
861	Vigilant	27990	14/2/1962	3/10/1971
862	Viking	27991	13/3/1962	3/10/1971
863	Warrior	27992	7/4/1962	26/3/1969
864	Zambesi[1]	27993	10/5/1962	27/3/1971
865	Zealous[2]	27994	28/6/1962	22/5/1971
Date of order 4/1959, Built at Swindon, Lot No 448				
866	Zebra	—	24/3/1961	1/1/1972
867	Zenith	—	26/4/1961	18/10/1971
868	Zephyr	—	18/5/1961	3/10/1971
869	Zest	—	12/7/1961	3/10/1971
870	Zulu	—	25/10/1961	28/8/1972

CHAPTER 9

THE HYMEKS

THE D7000 class, or Hymeks, were an innovation. They were the first, and only, type 3 diesel-hydraulics; they were the first diesel locomotives of any class for which the builder had acted as designer or had been associated as main contractor; they formed the first non-German installation of the Maybach 16-cylinder engine and K184 Mekydro transmission; they were built to a quite new design that was not an extrapolation of anything else that had gone before; yet 45 were ordered straight off the board, plus more before the first of the 45 was anywhere near completion. As engines, transmissions, axle drives and cooler groups were of types proved elsewhere, inability to have even a short testing time was accepted deliberately in order to get immediate advantage of more diesels in a situation where steam was going out rapidly. By and large the results warranted the policy, and the Hymek was a successful and popular type despite the troubles that came to it.

BTC orders placed were for 45 in June 1959, for 50 in July 1960, and for six in the winter of 1961–62. This was but a third of the 300 mentioned at an earlier stage and had led to the keen interest of Beyer Peacock (B-P); later BTC policy was to make up the required WR type 3 total with English Electric Co-Co diesel-electrics, partly because of numerous unbraked mineral trains down the Welsh valley lines. Tendered price was £80,000 each for the first 45, and £81,000 for the next 50.

The total of 101 diesel-hydraulics was put through the B-P books in five consecutive order numbers which did not line up in quantities with the BTC orders, and works numbers were consecutive only in two batches, with a gap between. Moreover, the Swindon lot numbers did not line up with any B-P variations, but only with the type of train heating boiler and brake equipment installed. First delivery was in May 1961, two months early; last delivery, in February 1964, was nearly a year after the first promised delivery date, but completion of some locomotives was held back while one or two troubles were sorted out. The first locomotive, D7000, was handed over at a small ceremony at Paddington on May 16 1961, when the WR chairman said the Hymeks would replace Hall and Grange 4-6-0s.

All diesel engines, including spares, were built by BSE under licence at the Ansty works, but the first 20 incorporated many parts made and machined at Friedrichshafen. Of the total of 116 sets of Mekydro transmissions, which included spares, 25 complete groups were made by Maybach and 91 by Stone, of which the first dozen or so to be put in were from Stone. All the Maybach-type axle drives (two C33 and two C33v in each locomotive) were made by Stone. Except for the Hardy-Spicer shafts to the dyna-starter and the hydrostatic pump for the fan, all cardans were of German Gelenkwellenbau (GWB) make supplied through Stone.

Stressed-skin principles of body construction as applied to the D800s, and sanctioned for the D1000s currently under design, were not adopted for the Hymeks. There was no need for them on the score of weight saving, and to have adopted them would have involved further licence agreements in K-M, and the adaptation of Gorton Foundry works procedure to an unfamiliar technique which would have increased the price and construction time. For a type 3 locomotive an adhesion weight around 75 tons all on, or 70 tons with tanks well down, was quite sufficient; it would permit a starting tractive effort of 45,000lb without reaching 30 per cent adhesion, and in a single-engined locomotive could be achieved easily with ordinary construction methods.

In practice, all-on weight in working order with full complements of fuel and boiler water was 75.5 tons and not the 74 tons usually quoted, with a maximum axle load of 19.4 tons; one bogie carried 38.1 tons and the other 37.4 tons; empty weight was 67 tons. With full tanks starting effort at 30 per cent adhesion was thus above 50,000lb; continuous rated wheel-rim effort was 33,950lb at 9.5mph. Change-over points of the Mekydro gear stages at full engine load and speed were 26, 42.5 and 70mph, and the proportions were so arranged that on the top step the efficiency curve would not have fallen below 80 per cent until a speed above 100mph was attained.

Though the principles of standardisation were found in the oil engine, as outlined in chapter 5, they were adopted nowhere else except in a general sense for the axle drives. The K-M-type

Above: *First of the Hymeks, set to work in 1961. In D7000-2 the warning horns were below the buffer beam*

British Railways

Right lower: *One of the second batch of Hymeks on a stone-train near Frome in 1967 after application of the BR reversed arrow symbol and blue paint. After D7000-2 all Hymeks had the Desilux warning horns above the cab-roof, protruding from the raised portion of the roof carrying the hatchways*

British Railways

Below: *Nearing the end of erection of the first group of 45 Hymeks at Gorton Foundry*

Collection D. Patrick

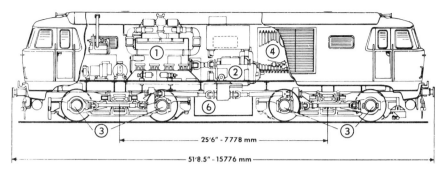

Above: Fig 13 *Layout of equipment, Hymek or*
D7000 class. Key:
1—Diesel engine
2—Hydraulic transmission
3—Axle drives
4—Cooler group
5—Train heating boiler
6—Fuel tanks

bogie was not suggested by either party; it would have involved B-P in negotiations with K-M and was not needed for a type 3 locomotive. The unsatisfactory riding at speed was not an influencing factor, for the speed of the D800s was only just being reduced to 80mph at the time of the first Hymek order, and the full importance of the problem was not then realised. The bogie put forward by B-P was cheap and effective.

No effort was made to standardise any mechanical components with those of existing WR diesel-hydraulics. In particular, the wheel diameter at 45in was different from the $39\frac{1}{2}$in

of the D800s and the 43in of the D600, D6300 and D1000 classes. Thus neither tyres nor brake shoes were standard, nor the axlebox make and journal size. Bogies were different from those of the D6300s though there were similarities in suspension. Thus the Hymek as a class was a cat that walked alone; fortunately for stores and spares there came to be 101 cats; and at the time of greatest tension in BR diesel locomotive history they were making a greater annual individual mileage than any type 3 diesel-electric. Certainly B-P never lacked confidence in its own design, and WR personnel usually had implicit faith in it, too.

Basis of the mechanical design was ordinary mild steel in standard-section rolled joists for the underframe and lighter standard angle sections for the body framing. Except for doors and removable hatches, the thin body plates were of steel and took no part in load carrying. Body and frame were welded, and few rivets and bolts were used. The well-known Commonwealth bogie was adopted, for it had given satisfaction on many tracks inferior to those of the WR in diesel locomotives and passenger rolling stock. In this bogie the swing link bolster was carried by triple full elliptic plate springs at each side; axleboxes were supported by long dropped compensating beams, between which and the underside of the cast steel bogie frames were the helical springs of the primary suspension. Because of the facility, in the design stage, of varying the length of the swing links and the unit deflection of two separate spring groups, plus some choice in the length of wheelbase, this type of bogie could be made a good rider over quite a range of speed and other conditions, and in the Hymeks it rode adequately up to 75/80mph. Axleboxes in this bogie were Timken taper roller type.

Main differences in the Hymeks as built were that the first 45, D7000–44, had the Vapor train heating boiler, Knorr type straight air brake with Laycock-Knorr compressor, and two Northey exhausters for the train vacuum brakes; D7045–

7100 had the Spanner mark IIIa train heating boiler, Westinghouse straight air brakes and Westinghouse compressor, and the same two Northey motor-driven exhausters as in D7000–44. All had a DP 216a-h battery. Like the other contractor-designed diesel-hydraulics (D600 and D6300 classes) sandboxes were on the bogies, and sanding was through electro-pneumatic valves.

Within the limits that were possible in a double-cab diesel locomotive, B-P, the BTC Design Panel and an outside consultant achieved a distinctive outline by a reverse-angle end contour that kept within the bounds of propriety and was not overdone like the Baldwin shark-nose end in the USA. Another innovation was a side-to-side lip wide enough to act as a footway above the buffers. Sometimes momentary doubt could arise as to whether a type 2 locomotive seen in the distance was a D6100 or D6300; recognition of a Hymek was instantaneous, and was helped by the off-white upper portion of the cab used from the beginning; it arose partly because each cab canopy was a complete fibreglass moulding. A lighter colour was kept throughout, though eventually it become yellow when end panels of that colour were adopted as standard.

When built, Hymeks were in the standard green; all eventually were blue, but none passed through the intermediate maroon stage. While green was still the base shade a broad band of

Left: *Maybach MD870 engine of the type used in
the D7000 Hymeks*

Motoren und Turbinen Union

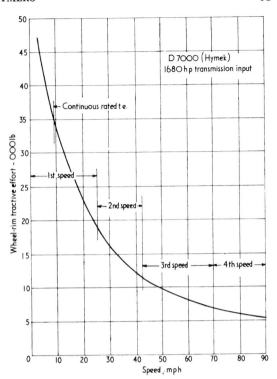

D 7000 (Hymek)
1680 h p transmission input

Right: Fig 14 *Speed/tractive effort curve of Hymek
locomotive*

grey-green ran along the body sides from end to
end at the valance. Numbers, in raised light alloy,
were fixed to each cab side, and below them was
the red circle denoting route classification—above
17.6 tons axle load. The BR emblem was in
transfer on each side in the centre; in later years
it was replaced by the reversed arrow symbol,
though this was not in the centre. A builder's
works plate was fixed to diagonally opposite cab
sides. The four-digit train indicator was different
from those on other WR diesel-hydraulics in
being a single unit, without the vertical centre
division into two parts, for here the base of the
nose was in one plate. With D7003 began the
mounting of the warning horns on the cab roof,
and this was followed in the D1000s, though
there was a light surrounding cowl. D7000–2 had
the horns below the buffer beam.

Origin of the type 3 diesel-hydraulic really
was the availability of the Maybach 16-cylinder
charge-air cooled engine (see chapter 5), which
made possible a single-engine locomotive with
hydraulic drive; a twin engine design would have
been uneconomic in this power range. In fact a
single-engine type 4 locomotive could have been
built with this engine taken up to its UIC rating
of 2000bhp. Despite the power margin, the
engine setting was brought down below 1750bhp,
that is, under the arbitrary limit adopted for
type 3. No BR power classification had been
allocated to cover a power range between 1751
and 1999bhp, and naturally no engine could be
set to an output for which there was no ticket.
Uusually 1700bhp has been quoted as the engine
output in the Hymeks, but Swindon records show
1740hbp at 1500rpm. Separate air intake filters
were used for the two pressure-chargers, and their
panels were staggered on opposite sides of the
roof curve, in which location they and the Vokes
air filters were well away from track dust.

Engine mounting was different from that of
preceding WR locomotives. A substantial carrying frame was welded to the locomotive underframe; on this the engine was carried through
eight Metalastik bearings, four per side, set

angle-wise to absorb both the engine weight and
the torque reaction from the crankshaft. This
system came into vogue in the early 1960s for
quick running lightweight diesels; it was known
as the chevron type, and the two angled arms
were on opposite sides of the engine. Centre of
the engine in the Hymeks was above the inner
axle of one of the bogies.

Engine speed control was of the Brush pneumatic type which permitted infinitely-variable
throttle opening and rotational speed; but the
control as a whole was electro-pneumatic, for
electric actuation was retained for the transmission valves, auxiliaries, and the safety and
warning systems. Most of the electric control
apparatus was within a dust proof casing on the
bulkhead of the A-end cab. Multiple-unit
coupling equipment was denoted by two small
yellow triangles on the buffer beam, but the
Hymeks could be coupled in multiple only among
themselves.

After 1956 Maybach never developed a bigger
engine or uprated an existing model unless it had
ready a Mekydro transmission able to absorb the
increased output; in this case the K184 model
was available. Its maximum input capacity was
1800hp plus, so that it could go with an engine
of 2000bhp. Though practically no small component was standard with any in the K104,

construction, operation, control and maintenance were simply on extrapolated lines. Mounting of the transmission block on the Hymek underframe was through three trunnion-type bearings without flexible pads. In its 'innards' the K184 had one difference from the K104; each claw clutch had an operating fork of its own, whereas in the smaller size each fork operated two claw clutches. This change involved a modification in the porting within the hydraulic control block, and an increase in the number of operating pistons; but each individual group to be moved at a gear change was of smaller mass than in the K104.

Dead central between the two bogies was the final output shaft of the K184U transmission; from this the drives to the two bogies were symmetrical. Each cardan shaft led to a C33v spur-and-bevel drive on the inner axle of the relevant bogie, and then a further cardan went at axle centre level to simple C33 bevels on the outer axle. Torque reaction arms attached to the axle drive casings were horizontal, and the reaction was taken up and cushioned by rubber cylindrical pads above the inner ends and secured to the cast steel inner transom of the bogie.

Size of engine and transmission, plus the restricted loading gauge and the wheel diameter chosen, led to such drive location problems that not a single cardan between engine and inner driving axle could be horizontal. With the engine mounted as close to the roof as practicable, the input shaft to the transmission still had to be above crankshaft centre line, which meant that the short primary cardan had to be angled upwards. Even so, the transmission output shaft was so low that, with the reduction ratio needed in the first axle drives, the two output cardans had

to be angled upwards. Underframe location, also affected by the chosen wheel diameter, prevented buffing shocks and drawbar pull being transmitted direct along the underframe, for the buffer height was below the bottom sill, and a dragbox had to be built up.

Of greater consequence in the end was that each of the two auxiliary cardan drives from transmission shafts, to the dynastarter and to the hydrostatic pump for the cooling-fan drive, were angled in two planes, horizontal and vertical, largely for reasons of space and to get some kind of through passage between the driving cabs. In practice nobody with any semblance to obesity could make that passage without contortions. Such a passage involved traversing the 18in space between the side-wall air-intake louvres and one of the offset radiator banks, across which, at full load, more than 30,000cu ft of free air a minute was passing. The other radiator bank was close inside the shutters on the other side, and so not only the fan but the whole cooling group was offset.

Distinct from the stressed-skin construction of the two leading WR type 4 locomotives, the more conventional body of the Hymeks was the better for some cross bracing between the two cab bulkheads, provided by putting the cooling group in a compartment of its own, with a hinged door in each end wall. The only other cross stiffening was by the irregularly spaced roofsticks. Sound insulation was applied only to the cab bulkheads and roof.

No tanks were supported by the roof. The two main fuel tanks were slung between the bogies with the main drive line running between them. The boiler water tank was in the body above the

transmission block; above it in, but not supported by, the roof was a small fuel service tank to which fuel was pumped from the main tanks, and from which a gravity feed led to the engine. All this meant that in full working order the underframe was carrying a dead load above 12 tons imposed midway between the two supports at the bogie pivots.

All Hymeks delivered up to February 1962 went first to Bristol Bath Road depot and worked miscellaneous services to Cardiff, London, Weymouth, Hereford and Shrewsbury. From March 1962 new allocations to Cardiff Canton were put on the South Wales to London expresses, normally four-cylinder 4–6–0 Castle class turns. These trains, loading up to 13 coaches of 450 tons, had to be hauled up the six miles at 1 in 100 out of the Severn tunnel followed by 11 miles up at 1 in 300 to Badminton. With these loads Hymeks could usually maintain a minimum of 23/25mph at the top of the 1 in 100, which was as good as a Castle and well beyond the capacity of a Hall or a Grange. 'Computed' performance for a Hymek on the West of England line was 490 tons London to Exeter at 60mph start to stop and without recovery margin, but only 280 tons on a 70mph timing, in this case with 20min additional recovery time recommended for any regular schedule.

Eventually the Hymeks worked over the entire WR system within the red circle classification, on all manner of trains from top-class expresses to demolition trains on the closed Somerset & Dorset section. They could run fast if conditions warranted. Among many records of the class in action examples show one maintaining 85/87mph along the virtual level between Twyford and West Drayton at the head of a seven-coach formation of 225 tons. Working solo one could also manage the 450-ton South Wales trains of 13 coaches along the level at 72mph, and take that load up two miles of 1 in 100 at 40mph minimum, and 11-coach loads of 380 tons down 1 in 1320 at 80mph; but all these feats were pushing things to the limit.

At the other end of the speed scale a handful of Hymeks was for some years employed banking on the Lickey incline, and up to three could be seen pushing at the tail of heavy northbound freights ascending the two miles of 1 in 37. For these banking duties the first speed stage of the Mekydro was locked out in case speed uphill got above 25/26mph, when there would have been a gear change and a momentary break in propulsive effort. This locking out meant the second speed stage was in constant use, and when banking freight trains might well be in the low-efficiency part of the converter curve.

When two bankers were used they could be coupled in multiple and driven by one man, but at one period three were felt to be needed behind ten or a dozen daily freights, and in this case the third locomotive had its own driver. Any unbraked uphill freight above 200 tons had to have a banker for braking reasons in case the train locomotive stalled and was unable to hold the train. Passenger trains of up to 10 or even 12 coaches of 400 tons went up unassisted if a type 4 diesel-hydraulic or diesel-electric was at the head. After the 1967 decision to prune severely the number of diesel classes running, the Hymeks were scheduled to be withdrawn by the end of 1973; this could not be achieved, and some were working well into 1974 as detailed in chapter 14.

Table XII—D7000 Class (Hymek) Locomotives, WR

No	works No B-P	to traffic Date	withdrawal Date of
Date of order 6/1959, Built by B-P, Order No 1711, Swindon Lot No 449			
D7000	7894	31/5/1961	30/7/1963
7001	7895	3/7/1961	
7002	7896	19/7/1961	3/10/1971
7003	7897	3/8/1961	1/1/1972
7004	7898	15/8/1961	16/6/1972
Date of order 6/1959, Built by B-P, Order No 1712, Swindon Lot No 449			
7005	7899	25/9/1961	2/7/1972
7006	7900	6/10/1961	11/9/1971
7007	7901	18/10/1961	19/4/1972
7008	7902	24/10/1961	1/1/1972
7009	7903	7/11/1961	6/5/1973
7010	7904	20/11/1961	1/1/1972
7011	7905	4/12/1961	
7012	7906	1/12/1961	1/1/1972
7013	7907	14/12/1961	1/1/1972
7014	7908	18/12/1961	1/1/1972
Date of order 6/1959, Built by B-P, Order No 1713, Swindon Lot No 449			
7015	7909	22/12/1961	7/6/1972
7016	7910	3/1/1962	
7017	7911	8/1/1962	
7018	7912	18/1/1962	
7019	7913	14/2/1962	15/9/1972
7020	7914	8/2/1962	1/1/1972
7021	7915	14/2/1962	1/1/1972
7022	7916	26/2/1962	
7023	7917	21/2/1962	6/5/1973
7024	7918	16/3/1962	1/1/1972
7025	7919	15/3/1962	1/1/1972
7026	7920	26/3/1962	
7027	7921	7/4/1962	29/11/1971
7028	7922	5/4/1962	
7029	7923	17/4/1962	
7030	7924	19/4/1962	6/5/1973
7031	7925	25/4/1962	11/5/1973
7032	7926	5/5/1962	6/5/1973
7033	7927	24/5/1962	1/1/1972
7034	7928	23/5/1962	1/1/1972
7035	7929	4/6/1962	1/1/1972
7036	7930	5/6/1962	9/6/1972
7037	7931	18/6/1962	15/9/1972
7038	7932	18/6/1962	2/7/1972
7039	7933	22/6/1962	3/6/1972
7040	7934	13/7/1962	1/1/1972
7041	7935	13/7/1962	1/1/1972
7042	7936	23/7/1962	1/1/1972
7043	7937	24/7/1962	1/1/1972
7044	7938	18/8/1962	6/5/1973
Date of order 7/1960, Built by B-P, Order No 1714, Swindon Lot No 455			
7045	7949	10/8/1962	11/11/1972
7046	7950	15/8/1962	1/1/1972
7047	7951	15/8/1962	1/1/1972
7048	7952	26/9/1962	1/1/1972
7049	7953	5/10/1962	1/1/1972
7050	7954	5/10/1962	1/11/1972
7051	7955	6/10/1962	1/1/1972
7052	7956	24/10/1962	30/11/1972
7053	7957	24/10/1962	16/4/1973
7054	7958	16/11/1962	30/12/1972
7055	7959	2/11/1962	
7056	7960	13/11/1962	1/1/1972
7057	7961	22/11/1962	1/1/1972
7058	7962	28/11/1962	3/10/1971
7059	7963	28/11/1962	3/10/1971
7060	7964	19/12/1962	3/10/1971
7061	7965	29/12/1962	1/1/1972
7062	7966	31/1/1963	3/10/1971
7063	7967	28/12/1962	3/10/1971
7064	7968	29/1/1963	3/10/1971
7065	7969	28/1/1963	1/1/1972
7066	7970	31/1/1963	29/11/1971
7067	7971	6/2/1963	3/10/1971
7068	7972	13/2/1963	30/12/1972
7069	7973	22/2/1963	3/10/1971
Date of order 7/1960, Built by B-P, Order No 1715, Swindon Lot No 455			
7070	7974	8/3/1963	8/9/1972
7071	7975	11/3/1963	1/1/1972
7072	7976	22/3/1963	3/10/1971
7073	7977	11/3/1963	10/12/1971
7074	7978	26/3/1963	30/12/1972
7075	7979	29/3/1963	6/5/1973
7076	7980	3/5/1963	6/5/1973
7077	7981	13/12/1963	2/7/1972
7078	7982	3/5/1963	3/10/1971
7079	7983	16/12/1963	3/10/1971
7080	7984	14/12/1963	7/11/1972
7081	7985	12/12/1963	11/9/1971
7082	7986	5/6/1963	19/4/1972
7083	7987	5/6/1963	3/10/1971
7084	7988	26/6/1963	11/10/1972
7085	7989	24/6/1963	11/10/1972
7086	7990	20/7/1963	1/1/1972
7087	7991	20/7/1963	7/10/1972
7088	7992	29/10/1963	1/1/1972
7089	7993	23/7/1963	6/5/1973
7090	7994	24/9/1963	12/6/1972
7091	7995	24/9/1963	10/8/1972
7092	7996	16/12/1963	20/6/1972
7093	7997	14/12/1963	
7094	7998	14/12/1963	1/11/1972
Date of order 12/1961, Built by B-P, Order No 1715, Swindon Lot No 457			
7095	7999	24/12/1963	16/10/1972
7096	8000	16/12/1963	30/12/1972
7097	8001	16/12/1963	30/12/1972
7098	8002	1/1/1964	30/12/1972
7099	8003	22/1/1964	15/10/1972
7100	8004	5/2/1964	1/11/1972

CHAPTER 10

D1000 CLASS

FEW WR men of more than 10 years' service can look back on the Western or D1000 class without regret and a feeling of 'might have been', for the whole project could have been a winner instead of a constant frustration. Some of the performances out on the line were superb; but until the final year or two the class was rarely out of trouble, poor maintenance and bad luck, and so was not dissimilar to several well-known steam types of this century.

In 1958 K-M rebuilt as a 3000bhp C–C locomotive a 96-ton 2200bhp locomotive of the same wheel arrangement originally built in 1957 as a 16-ton axle load demonstrator, mainly for the Jugoslav State Railways, and which in September 1957 had been examined in detail, and its performance sampled, by Grand, Hanks and Smeddle, and by R. C. Bond, BR's cme. The two Maybach MD650 engines and Mekydro K104 transmissions of 1957 were replaced by MD655 engines and K184 Mekydros, and a revised 15-notch BBC electric control system put in. In this new form the locomotive weighed 91.45 tons empty and 101.2 tons with 1100gal of fuel, 770gal of boiler water, and 1760lb of sand on board. Top designed speed was 87mph, and continuous rated drawbar pull 59,500lb at 12.3mph.

After putting up some notable hill climbing performances on the 1 in 40 north bank of the Semmering in Austria, on the 1 in 33 grades of the Mittenwald line in southern Germany and on the 1 in 50 sections of the Black Forest route, the locomotive, known as ML3000, then ran about 110,000 miles in daily mineral service with 2000/2400-ton trains over a 135-mile route with 1 in 125 ruling grade, followed by 150,000 miles on 500/600-ton passenger trains between Cologne and the East German frontier station at Helmstedt. By the beginning of 1963 it had covered 350,000 miles in service. It was opened up first after 85,000 miles to deal with a transmission bearing defect occasioned by a fractured oil pipe; thereafter the components were not opened up again for inspection until another 115,000 miles had been run, and after that a further 160,000 miles before the next occasion. At no time in this service, or afterwards, except during brief early trials in northern Germany with a dynamometer car, did ML3000 exceed 75mph.

Following trials and demonstrations in 1958, drawings and a specification of this locomotive were sent by K-M to the WR in accordance with a promise given to the Swindon chief draughtsman during a visit to Munich. When in 1959 greater power than that provided by the Warships was seen to be desirable for heavy trains on the London–Birmingham route, and for the faster schedules contemplated for the main lines of the Region as a whole, Swindon put in hand a design for a C–C in which two MD655 engines would be the basis of the power groups. To spread the work load over industry, and to maintain the principle of at least two suppliers, the transmission was of Voith type, with two of the then new triple-converter L630rV models, for in 45 Hymeks ordered four months before, large Mekydro drives had been specified; Maybach axle drives were adopted in the new C–C design.

When the D800 design was on the drawing board in 1956–57 the absolute minimum of change from the V200 design was made, and matters were left much to the WR. In dealing with the D1000 class the BTC cme of the time was shown as having definite overall charge, and the stated responsibility of Smeddle and Swindon was the 'detailed design and construction.' Mechanical layout of ML3000 could not be followed to any extent because of the restricted British loading gauge, a desire to decrease the noise level in the cabs which were not so well insulated as in Germany, and by the insistence of BTC central mechanical engineering on wheels 10 per cent larger than those of the D800s, though the axle load was seven per cent less; a different transmission was also adopted. One reason given for the enlarged wheel was to reduce braking heat in the tyres, as if the locomotives were intended for much use on heavy unbraked freights over steeply-graded lines.

From the time all this was realised, there was little further communication with K-M as the design developed, Swindon asking only for such drawings as it thought would be of direct use, and not calling on K-M as consultants as the licence agreement permitted, or sending over information as the design progressed. Incidentally, while Swindon was busy on the D1000

*Precursor of the WR D1000 class, the Krauss-Maffei ML3000 of 1958
which ran on heavy mineral and passenger trains on the German
Federal Railway; C-C axle layout, 3000bhp, 101 tons weight*

Krauss Maffei

design the DB and K-M were proceeding with a B–B of 2700bhp and 20 tons axle load, and a score were put into service through the winter of 1962–63.

Before the design of the C–C was complete in details the BTC in October 1959 placed orders for a total of 74, to be numbered D1000–73, of which 35 were to be built at Swindon and 39 at Crewe to Swindon-prepared drawings. This was not a departure from BTC practice, for the accelerated modernisation policy had already brought orders for several large batches of un-tried designs; but it *was* a departure in that Crewe had not previously built a diesel-hydraulic locomotive. A share-out of new work among BR shops was desirable and Crewe prices in general were lower than those of Swindon which were always on the high side. Prices for the Class 9 2–10–0 steam locomotives, for example, were 10 to 15 per cent higher at Swindon than at Crewe. Moreover, Crewe had a reputation for delivering on time, or close to it. In the case of the D1000s the original sanctioned price was £115,500 each from both works; the final price was some thousands more, but Crewe was still the cheapest in its costs.

Partly because of extra work thrown upon it, Swindon was slow in delivery after production had started, and the last five of the 35 allocated to Swindon were transferred at a late date (January 1963) to Crewe but still appeared before the last Swindon construction. Thus not only the scheduled D1035–73 came from Crewe but also D1030–34. Last locomotive of the 74 to be completed was D1029 from Swindon in

January 1964, but for three or four months thereafter was given over to the Research & Testing Section for controlled road and type tests, and was not put into revenue traffic until July 1964.

In addition to the tedious work that had to be done once again in designing and making within the BR loading gauge a stressed-skin super-structure, this time 65ft long in place of 58ft in the Warships, the 10 per cent stipulated increase in wheel diameter over that of the D800s and 15 per cent over that of ML3000, combined with engines and transmissions larger than those in the D800s, absorbed much time. Compared with ML3000 these factors brought a change in engine-transmission location, and a concomitant change in the drive distribution to the outer half of the bogie from the inner half. They also brought a greater static bending moment on to the superstructure between the bogies, and to what were perhaps less satisfactory cardan shaft installations.

Though the superstructure width and height were again 16in and 10in less than the Berne loading gauge followed by ML3000, the design changes noted plus the use of the rather heavier Voith transmission, made the body 1½ft longer than that of ML3000 and put up the empty weight by 7 tons to 98.4 tons. Fuel and water supplies were close in the two designs, and the all-on weight of D1000 as built was 108 tons. The basic model was 14 per cent lighter.

Over two years passed between the order and the completion of the first locomotive. This was not the fault of Swindon or Crewe. At Swindon

D1000 as it first appeared from Swindon painted in unlined desert sand colour, seen on a passenger train at Reading, January 1962. At diagonally opposite corners it carried a light alloy replica of the BR lion emblem British Railways

about ten locomotives were completed as far as they could go before the first main transmission blocks arrived. Being a new model of high capacity, German manufacture of the first few was deemed prudent, but Heidenheim was overloaded with work at the time and the delay caused much upset in Swindon erecting shop procedure and some at Crewe, and work had to be retarded. To proceed as far as possible wooden mock-ups of the Voith transmission blocks were made at Swindon and put in temporarily so that shafts, pipes, cables and connections could be brought up and made ready for the arrival of the real equipment. The first dozen or so transmissions went to Swindon on arrival. NBL also had put in hand a series of L630rV sets, but this was a new model for Glasgow and fresh tooling-up and production schedules were needed, so that the first sets from Queen's Park were not ready for despatch until March 1963. In the end, Heidenheim made 60 sets; NBL and Voith Engineering (Glasgow) Ltd built 103, covering 74 locomotives and 15 spare sets.

Main framing and superstructure, though technically on the same principle as those of the D800s, were to a slightly different contour; the body sides were slightly curved like a carriage, and cab shape, in essence, was the previously-rejected styled alternative put up for the D800. The same two $6\frac{1}{2}$in od longitudinal tubes and honeycomb arrangement of thin lateral and longitudinal plates topped by a floor plate were adopted, as was the strong double cantrail along each side. This structure, and the light girder-form roofsticks, made unnecessary any cross

partitions other than the cab bulkheads; as in the Warships internal electric lighting was good, and side window space was cut to a minimum, especially over the heavily loaded centre section.

Bogies were on the principle of those in the D800s, and, except for D1030–34, had the rubber-bushed linkage system of pivoting, with small lateral movement and cushioning. By the time construction of D1030–34 had been transferred to Crewe the revised bogie construction evolved at Swindon to overcome the riding troubles had been finalised, and these six locomotives had the revised design from new. Three axles in place of two in the D800s brought one further important change. The big axlebox arms supported at the inner ends on large bonded rubber bushed trunnions could not be applied to the centre axle, and so the two middle boxes had normal guides except that rubber pads were inserted behind the manganese steel liners. Another detail change from new compared with the D800 bogie was a large rubber block interposed on each side between the body bracket and the buckle of the large plate spring on each side. From this spring the body load was transferred to the bogie frame through the end hangers, which acted also as swing links, each with a top rocker arm bearing on the two helical springs. Later the large rubber block was removed.

Though of the same tread diameter as those in the D600s, 43in, the D1000 wheels had disc centres instead of the spoked form, and all had clasp brake blocks applied from four cylinders per bogie. The straight air brake was of Knorr type, with a Laycock-Knorr compressor, and

Left: *Front end of the first of the Western class as running in blue, with yellow end panels in 1971. Shed code plate above end footsteps*

British Railways

Below: Fig 15 *Layout of equipment, D1000 class.*
Key:
1—*Diesel engine*
2—*Hydraulic transmission*
3—*Axle drives*
4—*Cooler group*
5—*Train heating group*
6—*Fuel tanks*

Bottom: *First Crewe-built D1000, No D1035 Western Yeoman as turned out in July 1962*

British Railways

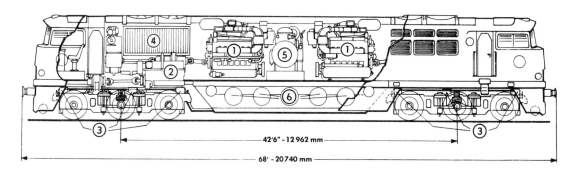

with two Westinghouse exhausters for the train vacuum brakes. Only the outer pair of wheels on each bogie was sanded, but in each direction; application was pneumatic, through flexible hoses from the boxes in the superstructure.

As usual in twin-engine installations the two power plants and their ancillaries were grouped symmetrically about the locomotive centre. Again as usual, the train heating boiler, here of Spanner mark III type, was off centre longitudinally and transversely, to give a side passage and a cross passage. As with other type 3 and type 4 diesels, various small auxiliaries and the need for diagonal symmetry in their location, prevented a clear internal passage all along one side, and a cross-over had to be made near the centre.

Flanking the central boiler were the two diesel engines. From them short cardans angled up to the transmission input. There was the same tightness to loading gauge height of engine-transmission combinations found in the Hymeks, partly because the Maybach pressure chargers had vertical shafts above the engine V and went well up into the roof. In MD655 engines the charge-air coolers also were at cylinder head level.

Standardisation of engine and transmission mountings between two makes was not imposed, because in neither case were economic alternatives available. The transmission block was carried through four Silentbloc mountings on the frame above the inner axle of the bogie, and a cardan shaft led from the output to a bogie-mounted distributor gearbox located between outer and centre axles. This had a step-up ratio of 1.38 : 1 that decreased the torque to be passed through the final cardans. From each side of the bottom of this box the final cardans were sloped down slightly to the C33v drives on the outer and centre axles, and from the latter a horizontal cardan led to the inner axle drive. This intermediate gearbox, as it had to transmit nearly 1100hp, was water cooled by a small bleed from the main engine-transmission water cooling system. Because of the required mechanical connection of all three axles in a bogie, axle drives had a pair of plain spur gears preceding the bevels. The intermediate gears and all axle drives throughout the D1000 class were made under licence by Stone.

Apart from its greater capacity, the Voith L630rV drive differed from the LT306r in the Warship and D6306 classes in that there was only one output flange, located at the opposite end to the input. The Mekydro in ML3000 had

the output below the input; and this, with the larger European loading gauge, meant that engine and transmission could be above the bogie, the intermediate gearbox between the centre and inner axles, and the cooling groups (lighter than the engine-transmission assemblies) in the centre of the locomotive, flanking the boiler. This could not be followed in D1000. Whatever the layout the space round the bogie top in a C–C was congested, and to do any appreciable work on the bogie the cardan from the transmission output to the intermediate gear had to be disconnected, together with sand pipes, speedometer cables and the like, the relevant end of the superstructure lifted up, and the bogie run out.

The UIC rating of the Maybach MD655 charge-air cooled engine was 1500 metric bhp, but this was reduced in the D1000s to 1380 British bhp at the same speed of 1500rpm, mainly because the maximum input capacity of the transmission was 1300hp. Nearly always D1000 class engine output has been given as 2700bhp, but Swindon records show 1380bhp per engine on top notch, or 2760bhp for the locomotive. All the MD655 engines for the 74 Westerns were built at BSE's Ansty works. Mounting in the locomotives was through four Metalastik feet angled to take torque reaction, and set chevron-wise.

Engine speed control was pneumatic and infinitely variable. It was on the same Brush principle as the Hymek control and many parts of it and the supplementary electric control for transmission and ancillaries were common to the two classes; the Westerns however were never fitted with multiple-unit control. On the occasions when two worked in tandem, or with a Hymek, each locomotive had its own driver. Engine and transmission characteristics and governing did not match up exactly and over the top half of the range in the second converter the full engine speed of 1500rpm was not possible, 1450/1460rpm being the average; this meant a drop of about 50hp in the locomotive output.

Combination of loading gauge limitations and the amount of heat to be dissipated (above two million BThU/hr per engine on full load on a hot day) led to each cooling group having two $42\frac{1}{2}$in roof fans, each with its own thermostatically controlled hydrostatic motor fed by a common hydrostatic pump driven by a cardan shaft and gearbox off one of the transmission shafts. The two fans in a group worked in parallel; maximum rotational speed was 1725rpm. Moveable shutters were provided outside the

Left: *Maybach MD655 12-cylinder engine as set to 1380bhp in the D1000 class. The two charge-air coolers are the two cubic boxes at the near, or free, end of the engine*

Motoren und Turbinen Union

Right: *Primary cardan shafts as used between engine output and transmission input of the D1000 class*

British Railways

Left lower: Fig 16 *Speed/tractive effort curve, D1000 class*

Right lower: *Three Westerns (D1027, D1014 and D1005) caught passing Bradford Junction, Wilts in June 1970. Two of the locomotives are being towed*

Ivo Peters

radiator blocks, operated automatically by small hydraulic cylinders. On the roof the two fan openings were crossed lengthwise by two angles with cross rungs to give a walkway and strengthen the cut out; in one form or another this was found in all WR diesel-hydraulics, but not always when new.

Against the all-on weight of 108 tons the starting tractive effort at 30 per cent adhesion

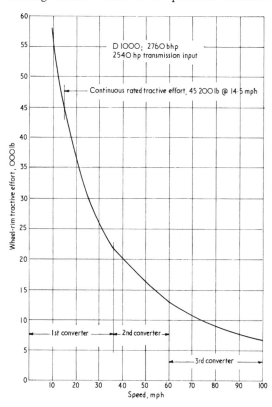

was 72,000lb; continuous rated wheel-rim effort was 45,200lb at 14.5mph, so the locomotives were quite suitable for the heavy stone trains from Merehead quarries, and the other heavy freights they worked in their later years. At top engine speed and power the converter change-over points were about 37 and 55mph, but at 90mph top the efficiency of the third converter was still above 80 per cent.

When built all D1000s had the WR atc apparatus. If a distant signal was clear a bell sounded in the cab; if at caution a siren sounded and a partial brake application was made; if the driver did not at once acknowledge the warning a full brake application was made by an emergency automatic brake (eab) valve, the action of which could not then be cancelled by the driver. Moreover power was cut off as soon as the train pipe vacuum fell to a predetermined value. The eab valve also functioned through use of the alarm signal in the train. In 1968–69 D1000s were dual equipped with the BR automatic warning system.

In 1968–69 all Westerns also were fitted with Westinghouse continuous air brake equipment to suit passenger trains of later mark II BR stock, which had begun to appear on the London–South Wales trains, and which at first had to be worked by diesel-electric type 4s already air-brake fitted. To fit in the extra equipment one of the end fuel tanks was removed from the honeycomb frame and a motor-driven Westinghouse compressor put in its place. Main air reservoirs were put inside the body alongside the engine carrying frames, which made passage along the interior still more difficult. The locomotives thus had Laycock-

Knorr straight air brakes, vacuum equipment for train brakes, and Westinghouse compressed air equipment for train brakes. Addition of the last-named apparatus plus the dual aws equipment put up the empty weight of a D1000 to 101.3 tons; but as the fuel capacity was reduced the full working order weight went up only to 109 tons.

D1000 began trials in November 1961, and when turned over to traffic at the end of December it was painted unlined desert sand; but with window corner pillars and recess black. D1001 followed in maroon and D1003–4 in standard BR locomotive green. These examples were used as the basis of a competition to establish future colours, possibly because the yellow end panels beginning to appear on various locomotives did not blend well with green. However, the next one or two Westerns to leave Swindon and Crewe

were painted green, but D1006 came out in maroon, and this was chosen as the future standard colour; it was eventually applied to all Westerns except, it is believed, D1036 which remained green until blue replaced maroon as the standard in 1967.

Nameplates were long light alloy castings at the centres of the two sides with polished name on black background in D1000, but with red background on green locomotives; number plates were similar castings on diagonally opposite cab sides; on the other side of each cab was a transfer of the BR coaching stock emblem, except on D1000 which had a light alloy simplified version of the lion in that emblem. The locomotives were unlined but apart from D1000 all had from new yellow lower end panels surrounding the train indicator frame. All locomotives also were turned out with electrification warning flashes on the

D1009 Western Invader *heads a Bristol–London train through Reading in 1964*
                                     Derek Cross

ends and against the cab doors. From 1967–68 the Westerns ran in blue until the end, with the BR coming-and-going symbol replacing the coaching stock emblems, with full yellow ends, and from 1968 with the data panel stencilled below each number plate.

Soon after introduction the early locomotives were put on two-day diagrams from Laira, covering a 700-mile round trip Plymouth–London–Wolverhampton–London–Plymouth; some even had three-day turns that covered the working on from Wolverhapton to Chester. The Birmingham Pullman service, with seven or eight normal Pullman cars, was handled when the fixed-formation diesel-electric sets were under repair. The D1000s also took up the principal services on the West of England and South Wales lines. As always intended, they were put on the hardest freight workings, and by 1964–65 about 25 per cent of the class mileage was being made on freight. The Birmingham express services were

taken over by D1500 diesel-electrics in 1964 and the D1000s were concentrated on the West of England, Bristol and South Wales routes.

The Westerns remained on top-class passenger turns to the end, but from 1969 took more and more freights, including the Merehead stone workings. These turns, and also the oil-tank trains to and from Dartford, were worked by Laira-based locomotives; indeed the class as a whole was always based on that major depot for Cardiff Canton did not give major diesel-hydraulic maintenance except to Hymeks.

With 500 tons of passenger stock a D1000 could climb the 1 in 80/90 up Wellington bank from Taunton at a minimum of 40/42mph; and with 550 tons could maintain 80/82mph along the level, 70mph up 1 in 265, and 60/62 mph up 1 in 115. The class coped with the constant time-table accelerations from 1964 to 1970, both with limited nine-coach formations and summer trains up to 14 or 15 vehicles, and were able to maintain the mile-a-minute timing of the Cornish Riviera to Plymouth. Until 1969 this run (then slightly slower) had two intermediate stops. The first section was the 142.75 miles from London to Taunton booked in 118min. Unchecked a D1000 could take 460 tons in this time, sustaining 85/86mph along the level, and never exceed-ing the statutory maximum of 90mph. With the lighter nine-coach load of 330/340 tons intro-duced in 1969, and a non-stop run to Exeter booked in 139min, two D800s were considered necessary at first, but a D1000 could keep this 74.5mph booking without trouble even if one or two pw checks were encountered.

Table XIII—D1000 Class Locomotives, WR

No	Name	Date to traffic	Date of withdrawal	No	Name	Date to traffic	Date of withdrawal
	Date of order 9/1959, Built at Swindon, Lot No. 450			1037	Western Empress	31/8/1962	
D1000	Western Enterprise	20/12/1961	11/2/1974	1038	Western Sovereign	7/9/1962	8/10/1973
1001	Western Pathfinder	12/2/1962		1039	Western King	7/9/1962	21/7/1973
1002	Western Explorer	19/3/1962	29/1/1974	1040	Western Queen	20/9/1962	
1003	Western Pioneer	14/4/1962		1041	Western Prince	10/10/1962	
1004	Western Crusader	12/5/1962	1/8/1973	1042	Western Princess	19/10/1962	21/7/1973
1005	Western Venturer	18/6/1962		1043	Western Duke	26/10/1962	
1006	Western Stalwart	6/7/1962		1044	Western Princess	12/11/1962	
1007	Western Talisman	1/8/1962	29/1/1974	1045	Western Viscount	16/11/1962	
1008	Western Harrier	4/9/1962		1046	Western Marquis	24/12/1962	
1009	Western Invader	24/9/1962		1047	Western Lord	4/2/1963	
1010	Western Campaigner	15/10/1962		1048	Western Lady	15/12/1962	
1011	Western Thunderer	27/10/1962		1049	Western Monarch	24/12/1962	
1012	Western Firebrand	17/11/1962		1050	Western Ruler	1/1/1963	
1013	Western Ranger	3/12/1962		1051	Western Ambassador	21/1/1963	
1014	Western Leviathan	24/12/1962		1052	Western Viceroy	4/2/1963	
1015	Western Champion	21/1/1963		1053	Western Patriarch	11/2/1963	
1016	Western Gladiator	16/2/1963		1054	Western Governor	2/3/1963	
1017	Western Warrior	15/3/1963	1/8/1973	1055	Western Advocate	2/3/1963	
1018	Western Buccaneer	2/4/1963	4/6/1973	1056	Western Sultan	8/3/1963	
1019	Western Challenger	2/5/1963	6/5/1973	1057	Western Chieftain	6/4/1963	
1020	Western Hero	21/5/1963		1058	Western Nobleman	25/3/1963	
1021	Western Cavalier	17/6/1963		1059	Western Empire	6/4/1963	
1022	Western Sentinel	16/7/1963		1060	Western Dominion	11/4/1963	17/11/1973
1023	Western Fusilier	23/9/1963		1061	Western Envoy	19/4/1963	
1024	Western Huntsman	1/10/1963	17/11/1973	1062	Western Courier	6/5/1963	
1025	Western Guardsman	1/11/1963		1063	Western Monitor	17/5/1963	
1026	Western Centurion	24/12/1963		1064	Western Regent	24/5/1963	
1027	Western Lancer	29/1/1964		1065	Western Consort	18/6/1963	
1028	Western Hussar	29/2/1964		1066	Western Prefect	14/6/1963	
1029	Western Legionnaire[1]	14/7/1964		1067	Western Druid	18/7/1963	
	Date of order 9/1959, Built at Crewe			1068	Western Reliance	12/7/1963	
1030	Western Musketeer	5/12/1963		1069	Western Vanguard	21/10/1963	
1031	Western Rifleman	20/12/1963		1070	Western Gauntlet	28/10/1963	
1032	Western Marksman	31/12/1963		1071	Western Renown	7/11/1963	
1033	Western Trooper	17/1/1964		1072	Western Glory	7/11/1963	
1034	Western Dragoon	15/4/1964		1073	Western Bulwark	3/12/1963	
	Date of order 9/1959, Built at Crewe, Order No DE286						
1035	Western Yeoman	27/7/1962					
1036	Western Emperor	29/8/1962					

[1] Ran from about 9/1967 with nameplate reading Western Legionaire

CHAPTER 11

DEVELOPMENT OF WR DIESEL TRACTION

GROWTH of diesel-hydraulic traction from the order for the first three D800s placed on Swindon in January 1956 began with the ensuing order in February 1957 for another 30 units on the same works. Before that second order was sanctioned by the BTC, and long before the first diesel-hydraulic locomotive of any kind came on to the region, the first seed for the complete dissolution of the new traction system had been sown with the retirement of Phillips on December 31 1956.

With him went the initiating, driving and central stabilising force, and there was no replacement. By that time the WR was committed to diesel-hydraulic locomotives, and substantial further orders were placed through 1957–60, but by the end of 1959 came a BTC decision to bring class D1 diesel-electrics on to the WR Bristol–Birmingham services, this before more than the first dozen Warships had the opportunity of showing their mettle.

No appraisal of diesel-hydraulic development and operation on the WR can ignore the hard core of opposition on non-technical grounds. This took two forms. First, that of the BTC and the successor BRB central mechanical-engineering department, committed from the beginning to heavy diesel-electrics with slow-speed engines,

and of the electrical industry and long-established sections of the oil engine industry. This opposition became strong in 1959, but as far as the railway side was concerned attained its peak in 1965 when attention was drawn to BR official figures that showed the Maybach-engined Warships and the Hymek locomotives were making bigger individual annual mileages than any diesel-electrics in the respective power classes.

Timing of this culminating opposition well after a top-level decision that no more large diesel-hydraulics were to be built coincided with a period when the D1 and D1500 heavy diesel-electrics hit the national headlines because of mass temporary withdrawals due to engine crank-case-frame cracks and numerous other defects. This moreover was after two or three years of D1 performance at an availability rarely above 60 per cent. Just at that time inner BRB circles were coming to realise also that the slow-speed engines of one of the principal diesel-electric type 2 classes would have to be replaced by another make, probably to the full total of 263, at an overall cost of around £5 million.

Second main ground of opposition was the intent at high level to eradicate from the WR that Great Western spirit of originality, independence and self-sufficiency, still marked 10 years after nationalisation, and to replace it by a less truculent and, if not national, at least more nationalised, outlook. WR management and personnel admittedly had done little in that decade to make their vitality impinge more tactfully on the 'national' situation at Marylebone Road, still ridden with power and prestige politics. There the WR management was considered arrogant and unco-operative. With faults on both sides, the psychological mutual opposition meant that certain advanced measures such as the old GWR automatic train control (later called the automatic warning system) and the diesel-hydraulics were pushed aside because of their origin, and something no better devised.

The decision, and, as high authority saw it, the needful and rightful decision, to bring the WR into national line was taken a step further by the translation of Grand, against his personal inclination, to full-time membership of the BTC in February 1959. He was replaced at Paddington for two brief years by J. R. Hammond, then WR civil engineer, who was moved on to the Eastern Region at the end of 1961 to make way for Stanley Raymond, who had an obvious remit to implement the decision fully. Raymond was then traffic adviser to the BTC, but his previous experience had been much in personnel management. Such policy could not take cognisance of special locomotives of good repute that formed no more than one-sixth of the total and were not liked at headquarters. The difficulties of Smeddle, who had come to appreciate the diesel-hydraulics greatly, were intensified. On his retirement at the end of September 1962, and the termination of Hanks's period of office as chairman at the end of the same year, no one was left in high position who had been in on diesel-hydraulics at the beginning and who knew just what the old WR management had set out to do.

Enthusiasm for diesel-hydraulics, and the desire to get the best out of their undoubted potentialities, centred after 1960 in Swindon works. There the employees, re-trained for, and gradually transferred to, general repairs of engines, transmissions and mechanical portions, took the diesel-hydraulics to their hearts, and worked on what came to be known simply as 'the

Maybachs' with interest and skill unabated until the high-level decision to close the works and do away with diesel-hydraulics. Especially was this so with the Swindon-built D800s and the Hymeks; the D1000 class for long remained a problem child.

Initial studies of 1954–55 had not led the WR management to expect any dramatic savings from diesel locomotive traction as a whole; the only direct economy anticipated was that from any increased availability of the locomotives. Even with this, the estimated reduction in system operating costs seemed modest, but the worsening coal situation, and its daily effect on operation, had to be countered by some other form of traction, especially as coal traffic itself was the biggest single source of WR revenue, and was declining without any new source of traffic on the horizon. In essence, accelerations and more efficient traffic operation were expected rather than a big cut in the financial deficit.

To give immediate effect to the terms of the modernisation plan, which suggested that areas should be turned over to diesel traction at a given time and with as short a turnover period as possible, the WR selected the whole area west of Newton Abbot as the first conversion scheme. This gave a compact district of about 225 route miles in which economies and system improvement could be evaluated clearly and reliably. Further, except for a few in South Wales, all the WR steep main line gradients were west of Newton Abbot, and diesels were felt to be suitable for those conditions. Estimates for this Devon–Cornwall conversion programme were around 130 locomotives, 70 of 2000bhp and 58 of 1000bhp, plus some dmu sets and shunters.

Large-scale diesel working was a feature of the modernisation plan, and after the diesel-hydraulics modelled on the V200 were sanctioned the WR had sufficient confidence to go into further details of the eventual conversion of the whole region in area by area change-overs, for electrification was not planned for any WR line.

Conversion area No 2 was centred on Bristol; it joined No 1 area working at Exeter, and covered the remainder of the London–Bristol–Taunton–Exeter trains, the west-to-north Bristol–Hereford–Shrewsbury–Crewe services, and various connecting lines. This conversion was expected to require about 200 diesels exclusive of shunters and dmu sets. It was to be followed by No 3 scheme, which included the Paddington–Birmingham–Wolverhampton main line and its offshoots and Shrewsbury–Chester–Birkenhead extension;

Above: *D816* Eclipse *heads a Plymouth–Penzance train off Brunel's Royal Albert bridge at Saltash in 1970. Locomotive in blue with full yellow end. The new road bridge is in the background*

British Railways

Below: *Manchester–Penzance train at Aller Junction about to ascend Dainton bank behind diesel-hydraulic D6300 and 4-6-0 No 5054* Earl of Ducie *in September 1959*

Derek Cross

London to South Wales passenger and freight services; South Wales to Midlands and North trains; and many South Wales district services. Finally would come the conversion of the remainder of the region.

Actual development did not follow entirely the intentions of the original planners, and at various times matters got out of step, and conversions of services to some extent replaced area change-overs. The carefully arranged procedure was somewhat disrupted when diesel-electric locomotives began to arrive in numbers, because the type of repair and maintenance naturally was different from that suited to the quick running lightweight components of the diesel-hydraulics.

No 1 conversion scheme was long delayed, partly by the protracted deliveries of pilot-order locomotives and those immediately following; in the event some steam locomotives continued to run in Cornwall until the beginning of 1962, and on the Exeter–Plymouth section until the autumn of that year. By that time clear-cut area conversions had become mingled with service change-overs to meet top-level directives for faster modernisation including greater mileages from the expensive diesels. Steam locomotive workings in general diesel areas were found almost to the end of BR steam in 1968, even though on November 27 1965 celebrations were held to mark 'Western

Farewell to Steam', when about 3000 steam locomotives had been retired and a £100 million diesel programme completed.

No 2 scheme was followed in the main, and involved the construction of a large diesel depot at Bath Road, Bristol, on which all the diesels in the area were based at first. No 3 conversion was to some extent anticipated, because from their introduction in the spring of 1962 Western-class locomotives based on Laira handled the London–Birmingham two-hour trains and some extensions on to Shrewsbury and Chester, and no more than inspection and servicing was given at Oxley, Wolverhampton. The diesel-electrics entered No 3 scheme in greater force, and at first were based on two large depots in South Wales, which also needed equipment and procedure to deal with diesel-hydraulics. To help in covering all 600-odd WR diesel locomotives with two kinds of transmission at work on the region by the end of 1963, additional maintenance facilities were installed at Old Oak Common (London), a provision unforeseen in the planning stage of 1955–56.

The careful organisation built up gradually to give efficient allocation, working diagrams and the handling of maintenance and repairs so that maximum availability could be obtained, was rarely kept unaltered for any substantial period, for BR was inherently unstable. After the policy decision to put diesel-electrics on to the WR among the diesel-hydraulics had become fully effective, alteration of regional boundaries brought the Southern Region's Waterloo–Exeter

line west of Salisbury into the WR from September 7 1964. The route was singled from 1967, for all traffic from London to Exeter and beyond was transferred to Paddington, and Salisbury–Exeter became a secondary line. The WR had to provide the motive power, and for ease in operation locomotives had to run through from Exeter to Waterloo, 172 miles, with a change of driver at Salisbury. D800s of Newton Abbot and Laira allocations were put on this service, and remained until the general withdrawal of that class in 1971–72. D6300s also worked over the ex-SR lines west of Exeter until they were closed.

Transfer of the Bristol–Birmingham working to the WR not only was the prime cause of the D1 diesel-electrics coming to the WR, but also brought the celebrated Lickey incline away from the LMR. After continuing with steam bankers for some years a handful of Hymeks was transferred to Bromsgrove to act in that capacity, and remained even after WR responsibility was cut back to the Bristol–Bromsgrove section.

Next disruptive effect was the transfer of all top-class London–Birmingham–Wolverhampton traffic to the then newly-electrified LMR, leaving the Paddington–Bicester–Birmingham route handling only intermediate traffic, though still with a few 60/62mph bookings. The diesel-electric type 4 class D1500s which had displaced the Westerns were no longer required from a power point of view, but remained on the WR for a few months longer until 15 were transferred to the LMR in the autumn of 1967 and replaced by an equal number of D800 Warships transferred to Old Oak Common. At the same time some of the English Electric type 3 diesel-electrics in South Wales were transferred to the Eastern Region and Hymeks were sent to replace them; from October 1967 all freight turns west of Swansea were diagrammed for Hymeks so that more type 3 diesel-electrics could be sent to the Eastern.

A cardinal point in WR plans for diesel traction had been accelerated passenger and freight services. Until 1964 the policy was more frequent trains at more or less existing end-to-end schedules but with additional intermediate stops. One case was the Paddington–Birmingham route, over which from September 1962 the service was increased to seven or eight two-hour trains a day in each direction, all with at least one stop, plus an additional non-stop train in 110min for the 110.9 miles. First of all the accelerations due to diesels, however, was that of The Bristolian from 105 to 100min in the summer of 1959; it lasted only the season and then was brought back to 105min when the civil engineer imposed a 90mph restriction on all trains and there was a lengthy bridge repair en route.

Revision of main line working ultimately was based on regular-interval services on accelerated schedules. In turn these were based on installed locomotive power and on locomotive and coaching stock diagrams to give good utilisation. Overall effect was to reduce both the number of locomotives and number of coaches needed to operate any line or group of lines. This was not peculiar to the WR; it was BRB policy, and was particularly apposite in helping to counter the sustained low availability of all locomotives, diesel-hydraulic and diesel-electric. On the WR this general revision, based on the maximum available outputs of the D1000 diesel-hydraulics and the D1500 diesel-electric classes, brought lighter trains, few outside the summer season having more than 11 coaches. Several subsequent very fast trains had a load limit of nine or ten.

Capacities of the first three Swindon-built D800s initially could be estimated only from what was known of V200 performance on the DB but Swindon research and development staff carried out on all main diesel classes controlled road tests on the principles evolved for the accurate assessment of steam locomotive performance. Broadly this method was based on the rate at which fuel was fed. After the tests, minimum point-to-point schedules for each class were drawn up for various loads on each route, on the basis of all-out working of the motive power, wherever running was unrestricted. Then certain margins were allowed for time recovery from out-of-course delays, bad weather and so on, and a definite schedule was offered to the operating department. The studies included computations to show the effect of various timings on fuel consumption.

D801 was tested in this fashion between Didcot and Bristol in October 1958 after running-in but before taking up normal service. Test trains varied from three to 15 coaches of 100 to 500 tons in weight; all were started on the 1 in 74 grade near Filton. Maximum speed attained downhill on the top power notch was 102/103 mph. Overall mechanical efficiency of the transmission between engine and axles rose to 82.5 per cent at high speeds, and this was fractionally lower than given by the ex-SR diesel-electric 10203 tested under similar circumstances.

The steep grades between Newton Abbot and

D825 Intrepid *leaves Buckhorn Weston tunnel
between Templecombe and Gillingham with the
10.20 from Exeter to Waterloo in February 1967*
Ivo Peters

Above: *Hymek D7075 shunting at Hapsford. near Frome, in 1966. On the right is one of the Whatley Quarry steam Sentinel locomotives*

Ivo Peters

Below: *D860* Victorious *climbs the branch from Witham with a train of stone empties for Merehead quarries in October 1970*

Ivo Peters

Plymouth were ever in the minds of WR men, and as sections of that line were liable to seasonal bouts of sea mist and hill mist a recommendation from the trials was that trailing loads between Exeter and Plymouth should not require more than 24 per cent adhesion, or 42,000lb from the D800s. This was enough to start a 500-ton passenger train on the ruling grade. For freight trains the criterion was not traction capacity but the holding power of a 20/25-ton goods brake van, which brought a limitation to about 325 tons on 1 in 50 whatever the type of diesel locomotive. In any case, because of three-link coupling strength no train unassisted in the rear was to require a peak drawbar pull above 44,000lb.

D800 itself had already shown its capabilities on the Bristol and West of England lines, but a result awaited from the controlled road tests of D801 was whether the class could be put on the Paddington–Birmingham two-hour expresses that stopped intermediately at Leamington Spa. Findings were that a schedule of 108min(61.7 mph) non-stop and without any recovery margin could just be kept with a clear road, and by using full engine power whenever running was unrestricted, with a trailing load of 360 tons. If a 120min non-stop schedule was in force, again without recovery margin included, the maximum trailing load would be 550 tons—a 50 per cent increase in load for an 11 per cent increase in time.

To cover weather and operating contingencies, to bring some economy in fuel, and to prevent the overall load factor being high enough to bring noticeable increase in maintenance and repair charges, the effective capacity of a D800 on the Birmingham route was settled at 368 tons on a 120min schedule which included 12min recovery allowance. This was not enough for D800s to be allocated regularly to the service but it was close enough for them, at a later date, to be accepted as emergency replacement power for a defective D1000 or D1500. For a period a D800 did work regularly one of the Birmingham trains which had loading conditions easier than normal. The two-hour timing with a 133-ton 2000bhp diesel-electric was with a maximum trailing load of 328 tons, so the early belief of WR management that diesel-hydraulic might be a coach better than a diesel-electric on fast timings was substantiated.

Perhaps the computed load and timings worked out for D800s and D1000s were accepted without further consideration by the operating department, for some of the fastest schedules introduced

in 1966 were eased a few minutes the next year, though subsequently some were once again accelerated. In general, allowing for delays en route, the combination of schedules and loads called for a good deal of full-power working, and the daily load factors were higher than any normally put upon the V200s in Germany. Computed performances of a D800 London to Exeter were 640 tons at 61mph average and 480 tons at 65mph.

The 1966 peak was a 78.2mph run over the 94 miles from Paddington to Chippenham but a harder duty was the eastbound Golden Hind from Taunton to Paddington, 142.75 miles in 127min, or 67.45mph, and a minute longer in the opposite direction. Next year the Paddington–Chippenham speed was eased to 75.16mph, but the best London–Taunton time was reduced to 123min and to 122min in the reverse direction. However, in 1968, with increasing use of and better performance from D1000s and D1500s, and limited use of two D800s in tandem, the Paddington–Taunton times were cut to 118/120 min and to 122min eastbound. For the first time came a regular 60mph booking between London and Plymouth. Also for the first time 70mph schedules came to the West of England line; hitherto all WR 70-plus start to stop timings had been along the Bristol and South Wales lines.

Despite faith in computed schedules, before the Golden Hind began to run in June 1964 on a 230min timing to Plymouth and 235min in the reverse direction, with three intermediate stops each way, a special trial ran on April 8 that year in which D1027 at the head of seven coaches, and allowed a maximum speed of 95mph, ran the 225.7 miles to Plymouth non-stop in 208min including a long pw slack; in the reverse direction it ran from the Taunton start to London in 113 min, or 75.8mph start to stop. A speed of 76.5 mph was maintained up 1 in 115, 66mph up 1 in 90, and 36mph up the 1 in 36/40 of Dainton bank. Almost coincident with this run, D1023 made a special return trip between London and Bristol in which the 106.7 miles to Bath occupied 89min 30sec start to stop; including a 2min halt at that place the whole 118.3 miles to Bristol were covered in 105min, that is, to the schedule of The Bristolian but with 420 tons trailing in place of the normal 260-ton formation of the service train.

On 70mph bookings over the West of England line the D1000s were not fully extended with nine coaches, but in the mid 1960s these locomotives were not running well enough for a whole

D831 Monarch *and D808* Centaur *coupled in
multiple-unit leave Westbury with the 14.30
ex-Plymouth to Paddington in July 1968*

Ivo Peters

70mph timetable to be drawn up on them. On unchecked runs, and in good condition, they could keep a 123min(70mph) booking from Taunton to London with 500 tons, though then there was no margin in hand, and the engines were worked flat out in maintaining 70mph up 1 in 265, and 85mph down the infinitesimal slope of 1 in 1320. Such combinations of load and speed involved fuel consumptions far above the 1.0mpg with which the 315-ton Cornish Riviera was worked non-stop to Plymouth on the 240min 56.5mph schedule in force when diesels were first used on that train in 1958.

Use of the Western and Warship diesel-hydraulics (and later of the allocated D1500 diesel-electrics) permitted a speed-up of the whole region as envisaged by the WR in 1955, and possibly to an even greater degree than then contemplated. By the summer of 1968 there were 23 daily runs above 70mph start to stop, though two or three were made by the diesel-electric Pullman sets, and 200 daily runs at speeds of a mile a minute to 68mph. They were not confined to Bristol and West of England lines, for there were 70/72mph trips from London to Newport. Even the Hereford West-to-North line had its

60mph timings, as had the Paddington–Birmingham line, by then demoted to a secondary route and operated by D800s. Yet a further speed-up was effected in 1969, when 37 daily journeys, including the Pullmans, were at start-to-stop averages above 70mph, and 285 journeys were above the mile a minute rate.

When the very fast schedules were under consideration doubt arose as to whether the 2270bhp of the 37 Maybach-engined Warships and the 2760bhp of the Westerns and 2500bhp of the derated D1500s would be sufficient. This led to the staging of a trial on June 3 1965 to determine whether 75mph schedules were at all feasible. Two English Electric type 3 diesel-electrics, D6881–2, of Co–Co layout and 1750bhp apiece were coupled in multiple to give 3500bhp, and ran from London to Plymouth and back with an eight-coach train of BR's prototype XP64 stock plus a dynamometer car, weighing 350 tons. Westbound the train ran via Westbury and covered the 173.5 miles to Exeter in 132min 18sec, or 78.6mph, with a peak of 92mph. The eastbound train came back from Taunton via Bristol and Bath and stopped only at Bristol between Plymouth and London, making succes-

D7001 crosses Pensford viaduct with the 18.00
Portishead–Radstock coal empties in June 1968
Ivo Peters

sive non-stop runs of 127.6 and 118.3 miles. On the latter section the train made the fastest time ever recorded between Bristol and Paddington, 86min 36sec, equal to 82.6mph average, and with 100mph attained on two lengths. The extraordinary motive power chosen for this round trip may have owed something to the then regional general manager, G. F. Fiennes, appointed a short time before from the Eastern Region. The same locomotive combination was used on a few regular trains for a week or two afterwards but motive power acquired specifically for Welsh Valley coal trains was not practical railroading on first grade expresses.

Shortest time recorded between Bristol and London with only one locomotive at the head of a regular train seems to have been the 92min 52sec of D804 *Avenger* on the inaugural eastbound run of The Bristolian on its 100min schedule on June 15 1959. This seven-coach train ran via Filton and Badminton, and not via Bath; mileage of this route is 117.6. In those early days of the four-axle Warships there was no restriction of top speed, and D804 reached 100/102mph at three separate points with a trailing load of 260 tons (246 tons tare). Three pw slacks

were encountered, two of them to 15mph at locations where speed normally would have been in the 80s; and the net time was within half a minute that of the unchecked run of the two type 3 diesel-electrics, which ran over a route 0.7 mile longer. The Bristolian, as far as the locomotive was concerned, was part of a round trip diagram between Plymouth and London.

A succession of exploits of this order from the first dozen or so D800s in 1959 gained the class an appreciation by WR men generally that was never lost entirely. With Bristolian loads 75mph could be sustained up 10 miles of 1 in 300, and as much as 95mph along the level. The class was not confined to lightweight trains, and along the main lines in 1959–62 was expected to take whatever load came up. On fast trains the loads were usually within 340/360 tons, and 400 tons in summer. Between London and Newton Abbot, with a ruling grade of 1 in 80/100, an end to end average of 55/56mph including one or two stops could be maintained. With 300/325 tons 22/25mph minimum could be kept up the 1 in 37/56 to Dainton, and 30/32mph up the 1 in 60/80 grades in Cornwall. When schedules called for it, 45mph could be maintained up 1 in 75

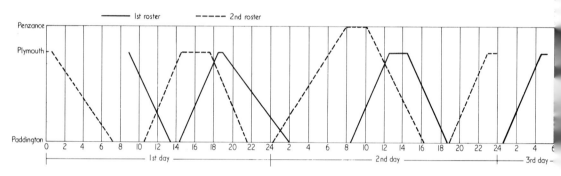

with 260 tons. Over all of these services the average fuel consumption of the D800s through 1960–61 was 1.0mpg. Trains of 400 tons trailing could be started on 1 in 40 on notch 5, and only with the train well under way was a move to notch 6 needed to continue the acceleration up-hill.

Such celerity as that of *Avenger* was not allowed for long. By the end of the summer of 1959 the WR civil engineer imposed the ceiling of 90mph for all types of locomotive, and this called for harder work uphill if time was to be kept on 65/70mph schedules. When in 1960 the maximum permitted for D800s was dropped to 80mph because of riding, timekeeping on schedules of 65mph or more was possible only with a clear road throughout. The class was unaffected in heavy train haulage at averages up to a mile a minute, and 420/450-ton trains could be taken from London to Chippenham in 84/85 min for the 94 miles.

In 1968 the Cornish Riviera under diesel-hydraulic haulage came down to $3\frac{3}{4}$hr (60mph) between London and Plymouth, though with the traditional non-stop run eliminated and stops at Taunton and Exeter inserted. Load limit was 11 coaches of about 390 tons. A revision the next year cut out the Taunton stop, and quickened the schedule to $3\frac{1}{2}$hr, with the load limited to nine coaches taring 320 tons. The London–Exeter part of the run was made in 139min, equivalent to 74.9mph. This schedule was part of an overall time of 6hr over the 305 miles from Paddington to Penzance. Two Maybach-engined D800s in multiple-unit were employed for the whole run and gave 4540bhp at the head of the train, more than sufficient to keep any schedule permitted by the track alignment and the permissible top speed of 90mph. Such twin-unit power was used also on other and heavier trains such as the 14.30 Paddington to Penzance, which as far as Newton Abbot could load up to 14 or 15 vehicles weigh-

Above: *D1006* Western Stalwart *propels a load of stone out of Merehead quarries as D7041 (left) arrives with a train of empties*

Ivo Peters

Left upper: *A D800 Warship leaves Barry Docks with a train containing over 10,000 bags of flour and animal feed destined for Plymouth and Cornwall*

British Railways

Left: Fig 17 *Two-day rosters for multiple-unit D800s in 1968*

ing 450 to 500 tons. The twins had no difficulty in maintaining 90/92mph along the level with 350 tons trailing, reaching 90mph in seven miles from the Paddington start, and maintaining 82/85mph up 1 in 115. Their principal advantage was ability to keep time despite several out-of-course delays.

Multiple-unit working with four pairs on regular diagrams and others available for certain turns lasted only a year; in the 1969 timetables only two pairs were diagrammed daily and were confined to the Cornish Riviera service. The two 48-hr rosters of twin-unit D800s from Laira as followed in 1968 are shown in Fig 17. Only once included a through locomotive run between Paddington and Penzance, but certain other diagrams involving single locomotives had such runs. The recast timetables of 1969 separated completely the Torbay and Plymouth/Cornwall services, and as each ran at alternate hours it was possible to keep trains to eight coaches (Torbay) and nine coaches

(Plymouth), and were thus brought within the capacity of D1000s working solo. Trains of 10 to 12 coaches could be taken at peaks without double heading, but D1000s were hard put to keep 122min up from Taunton with above 450 tons.

From 1968 diesel locomotive crew rosters were changed; long through runs and lodging turns (the latter known as double-home workings) were eliminated. No longer did Old Oak Common drivers take the trains through to Plymouth, or Laira men drive all the way up to London, as was common in the steam days and through the first decade of diesel working. All West of England passenger trains were given a crew change at Taunton or Exeter, still with drivers from Old Oak and Laira, but the former men henceforth did not work west of Exeter or Laira men east of Taunton, though a few duties involved Laira men going north of Taunton to Bristol. These changes applied also to locomotive crews of sleeping car and Motorail trains not publicly advertised to stop at Taunton.

Apart from the regular twin-unit D800 workings of 1968–69 unusual combinations could be seen at times and because of multiple-unit control limitations were not always in the charge of one driver. On a few occasions three D800s could be seen on 14- and 15-coach West of England trains, with the two leading units multi-coupled and the third unit with a driver of its own. Now and then in Cornwall two D6300s could be seen piloting a D600, and again one driver was at the

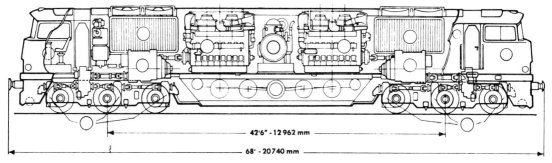

42'6" - 12 962 mm

68' - 20 740 mm

Fig 18 *Layout of 4000bhp C-C diesel-hydraulic locomotive proposed for Western Region early in 1963*

front and another on the third locomotive. Two
Westerns, or a Hymek and a Western, needed
two drivers, for the Westerns had no multiple-
unit control.

Had the engines in the D1000s been set to the
UIC rating of 1500 metric bhp (1475 English
bhp), or even to the BS rating of 1445bhp, the
extra 130/190bhp in the locomotive might have
obviated all thoughts of coupling two type 3
diesel-electrics or two D800 diesel-hydraulics.
The high power question might have had an
interesting sequel for in February 1963 Maybach
sent to the BRB a general arrangement drawing
of a 120-ton 4000bhp C–C diesel-hydraulic locomotive with standard well-proved engines and
transmissions. It was not even acknowledged.
Constructional lines were to be similar to those of
the D1000s; engines and transmissions were to
be duplicates of those in the Hymeks but with the
engines set to the UIC rating of 2000bhp apiece;
and as shown in Fig 18 the overall length would
have been no more than that of the D1000s. The
only result of this proposal was that shortly
afterwards designs for single slow-speed engined
diesel-electric locomotives of 4000bhp began to
circulate.

CHAPTER 12

DEPOTS AND WORKSHOPS

BECAUSE of the use of lightweight quick-running engines and non-electric transmissions, maintenance and servicing procedure on the WR differed in some degree from that on other regions, for it was based on unit-replacement technique. Swindon works did all major repairs to diesel-hydraulics; in early stages, before any large depots were fully equipped, it dealt also with engine and transmission-block changing but this, plus visits for accident repairs and design modifications, tended to bring locomotives to Swindon more frequently than desirable. Therefore, viewing the WR as a whole, two main depots at Plymouth and Cardiff were agreed, which between them would have the allocation for heavy maintenance of all locomotives.

Beneath these two centres in status were four large depots which undertook periodic maintenance as well as lighter maintenance, inspection and servicing; they were at Newton Abbot, Bristol, Landore and London, all on the sites of old steam depots. At Old Oak Common (London) some major maintenance on type 2 locomotives was to be done, as well as planned maintenance on type 2, 3 and 4 locomotives; until the LM Region took over the principal London–Birmingham services some work also had to be done on large diesel-electrics.

Location of these six main centres entirely in the south is explained by the transfer from the WR to the LMR by 1963 of the Birmingham–Chester–Birkenhead line and the ex-Cambrian system north of Aberystwyth. Despite the addition of the ex-Southern Region lines west of Salisbury in 1964, these transfers meant the WR mileage when the diesel programme was complete was only 2700 against 3000 in 1955.

Purely servicing and daily inspection points to deal with a few type 2, 3 and 4 locomotives were located at numerous points in Cornwall, Devon and the West Midlands. Such facilities for locomotives were added to the big dmu depot at Reading. None had actual locomotive allocations. All locomotives, diesel-hydraulic or diesel-electric, were based on the six establishments listed above. This allocation was made on maintenance requirements, as a compromise between cyclic operation and tying locomotives rigidly to a servicing depot.

Traffic and regional alterations during the 1960s brought changes to this organisation. Newton Abbot was demoted, for there was no need for a maintenance depot so close to Plymouth. On the other hand the traffic in South Wales warranted another depot that could do some maintenance and relieve Cardiff and Landore; facilities were thus provided at Ebbw Junction in 1965. The various establishments and their categories as they were at the beginning of 1974 are shown in Table XIV.

Enginemen were not confined to these six depots and were located at many other places. Where there had once been steam sheds, and at certain other strategic locations, such as marshalling yards men now booked on and off at stations. Driver training was given under the direction of one or other of the six main depots, though often out at one of the servicing stations; at some places concurrent instruction was given on both diesel-electric and diesel-hydraulic locomotives. WR men also were given instruction on

Table XIV—WR Diesel Locomotive Depots

District	Location	Maintenance	Servicing	Fuelling
London	Old Oak Common	*	*	*
	Ranelagh Bridge (Paddington)			*
	Southall			*
	Reading		*	*
	Oxford		*	*
Bristol	Bristol Bath Road	*	*	*
	Exeter			* S
	Gloucester		*	*
	Plymouth Laira	*	*	*
	Marsh Jct.			
	Newton Abbot		*	*
	Penzance		*	*
	St Blazey		*	*
	Swindon		*	*
	Taunton			* S
	Westbury		*	*
	Worcester		*	*
Cardiff	Canton (Cardiff)	*	*	*
	Ebbw Jct.	*	*	*
	Hereford			* E
	Landore	*	*	*
	Maliphant			*
	Margam		*	*
	Severn Tunnel Jct.		*	*

E Emergency fuelling only
S Fuelling for shunters only

Above: *A Hymek passes through the photo-electrically operated vertical-brush washing machine outside Newton Abbot depot*
British Railways

Right: *Interior of Laira depot in 1962, with D6300s and D800s in the bays*
British Railways

Below: *General view of Plymouth Laira depot, then dealing solely with diesel-hydraulic loco-motives on the maintenance side*
British Railways

type 4 diesel-electrics at Old Oak Common, and at the Tyseley depot in Birmingham, the latter by then transferred to the LMR.

Heavy or scheduled repairs to WR large diesel-electrics were not done at Swindon, but at Crewe and Derby, to which the 120 English Electric type 3 and nearly 200 Brush type 4 loco-motives were taken at appointed times or when out-of-course events or design defects made a visit necessary. Attempts were made to introduce a unit replacement system at WR depots in South Wales to reduce the time out of service needed by a trip to Derby or Crewe, but the size and weight of the engines and main generators, and the crane capacities and roof heights at WR depots laid out for diesel-hydraulics, did not per-mit this idea to be carried very far. At the time

when the WR had its maximum allocation of diesels of all types, about 45 per cent of the number had to be taken away from the region for planned heavy repairs and design modifications.

Changes of engines, transmissions and bogies of diesel-hydraulic locomotives at Plymouth (Laira) and Cardiff(Canton) major depots needed a pre-reference to shopping control at WR headquarters, because in general those two establishments did not hold spares of the large assemblies, which had to be sent from Swindon. According to the work load, the location of the unit when failure occurred, the type of failure, and the general motive power position, a more expeditious solution might be to send the whole locomotive to Swindon.

To cater for the No 1 conversion scheme work was put in hand first at Newton Abbot depot. This location had the advantage that the high power diesels allocated to it could build up big mileages on long distance fast passenger trains to London and Bristol, as Devon-based steam locomotives had done for years. Subsidiary service locomotives and dmu sets would also work east of Newton Abbot at least as far as Exeter. However, after no more than a handful of diesels was in service, a decision was made to build a new large diesel depot on the site of the steam shed at Laira in the eastern suburbs of Plymouth, from which the diesel locomotives would have the same range of operation eastwards, and which would handle everything but major repairs.

Newton Abbot then became a secondary diesel depot; it retained some of its steam buildings refurbished for diesels, and the new servicing and oil storage equipment was alongside. As late as 1963 a new automatic washing plant was put in, with photo-electric control of pump switching and of brush and jet operation. Today Newton Abbot does only a certain amount of servicing and fuelling.

An early (1960) proposal to adapt the old Stafford Road locomotive shops and sheds at Wolverhampton for the repair and maintenance of diesel locomotives was put aside because of the coming transfer of all WR territory in the area to the LMR. Only light servicing facilities were put in at Oxley shed in the neighbourhood, and they soon came under the supervision of Tyseley depot, taken over by the LMR.

Plymouth Laira was the general prototype of WR large diesel depots, and initiated on that region the standard side-by-side location of servicing and maintenance shops, and in some respects followed practice already established on BR, and, for example, on such other railways as CIE at Inchicore. Partially opened in 1960, the Laira scheme was completed in 1961; until that time many minor repairs had to be done at Swindon. Long after the diesel sections were in operation Laira continued to give some servicing to steam locomotives coming into the area with summer trains from east and north of Exeter which lasted until the autumn of 1963.

Laira was intended for all three classes of work on diesel-hydraulic locomotives, but on dmu sets did only maintenance; servicing was done a mile or two away at Belmont. Buildings were framed in reinforced concrete, with barrel vault roofing, and

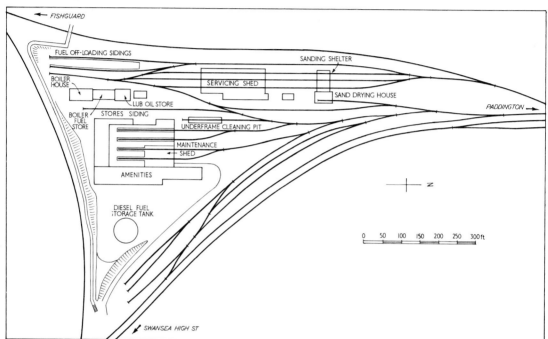

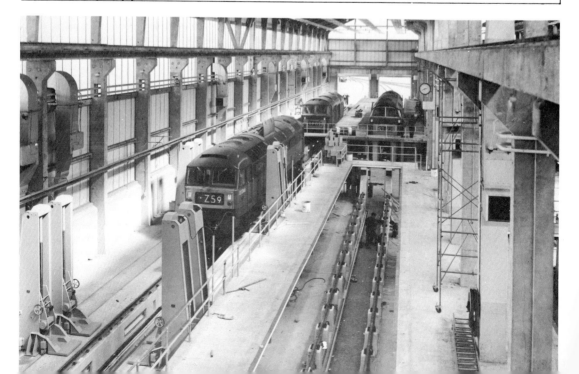

Top: *Exterior of Cardiff Canton depot for diesel-hydraulic and diesel-electric locomotives at the time of its opening in 1964*
British Railways

Centre: Fig 19 *Ground plan of Landore diesel depot*

Bottom: *Maintenance shop at Cardiff Canton. On the left is the one through track, equipped with several pairs of synchronised lifting jacks. Locomotive nearest on left is a D1500 diesel-electric; behind it is a Hymek, and to the right a D1000*
British Railways

patent glazing on the side walls to give maximum daylight. In the maintenance section were two 280ft pits with sunk floor and high level platforms for locomotive work, while another three 210ft pits and tracks were allocated to dmu work. In the cleaning and servicing shed were three 140ft pits. Facilities for bogie changing were included, and a tyre-reprofiling machine. Offices and staff amenities were in a two-storey building. Fuelling and sanding points in the yard had glazed reinforced concrete shelters. Fuel storage totalled 45,000gal. Being on marshy ground all the main buildings and the main fuel storage tanks were erected on piles. Some heat for the buildings was generated in boilers fuelled with waste sump oil from the motive power.

By the time reconstruction of Laira was advancing a further diesel depot was open. This was Bath Road, Bristol, closed to steam on 12 September 1960, by which time some of the diesel handling equipment was in place. Rebuilding was accelerated immediately afterwards, but the installation was not complete by the time the first Hymeks arrived. The first six D1 diesel-electrics allocated to the WR for the Bristol–Birmingham service had to be handled for a while at Bristol St Philip's Marsh steam depot until Bath Road was ready for them. Bath Road took a maximum of 45 Hymeks and some of the D800 Warships.

For the diesel turnover in South Wales, with a large number of type 3s needed for short-distance mineral traffic, Landore was in operation well before Cardiff Canton. It was located in the triangle between the two approaches to Swansea High Street station from the Cardiff–Fishguard main line, and had entrances from the main line and from the eastern exit from High Street. It was opened formally when D1061 broke a tape

on 3 May 1963. Planned ultimate capacity was 93 type 4 and 25 type 3 diesel-electrics and 37 type 3 diesel-hydraulics, plus 20 of the three-axle type 1 BR diesel-hydraulics of 650bhp. At opening the depot had an allocation of 45 type 4 and a dozen type 3 diesel-electrics, plus 33 Hymeks.

Standard three-axle 350bhp diesel-electric shunters also were given maintenance, but in general came to be serviced at a plant against the new Margam marshalling yard where most were engaged in shunting. Later Margam dealt also with the servicing of line-service locomotives. Landore's first allocation, along with local dmu sets, ensured full diesel working west of Swansea, as well as much freight and passenger working in Glamorgan; when the full allocation was received 15 steam sub-sheds were closed.

As shown in Fig 19 three roads with a sanding cover led into the heated servicing shed, which had capacity for two locomotives on each of the three tracks. These tracks had illuminated pits below and fuelling connections at the sides, along with electric power and compressed air connections. The 70,000gal overhead fuel storage tank was outside, well away past the maintenance building, with underground pipes from the tank wagon reception and unloading bay to the service shed points. After servicing and preparation a locomotive moved on through the shed and reversed down the exit road, passing through a standard vertical-brush washing machine operated photo-electrically.

The maintenance building was entered through power-operated roller type doors, and had four stub-end roads in two bays, each with a 150ft pit 4ft deep. It was heated by air circulation and electric roof panels, and ventilation was by rotary extractors in the roof which drew out diesel exhaust fumes. Here the floor was sunk, and the whole of one bay and half of the other had fixed high level platforms, so that locomotive equipment at all heights could be reached and handled. The other half of the second bay was provided with portable platforms. No fuelling was done here, but lubricating oil supplies were piped in from the outside tank, and power and air points were distributed. Hot water washout points enabled engine cooling systems to be flushed and refilled with hot water so that no time was lost in cooling the engine down. Only one bay had a crane, of 3 tons lifting capacity, and this was enough for the sub-assemblies the depot was allowed to change. Air filter cleaning and recoating were done in a separate room at sunk floor level, where sump oil samples also were checked.

Above: *Interior of Old Oak Common depot. Nearest the camera is one of the D6300s allocated to the Paddington empty stock workings; behind it is a Hymek of the first batch*

British Railways

Below: *Inside Swindon works September 1959, showing the replica of the old 2-2-2 North Star alongside D812 and D813 almost complete*

Ivo Peters

Partly due to accelerated modernisation activities the arrangements for Cardiff Canton major depot were disjointed for an establishment involving an outlay exceeding £1 million. The decision to make the second major depot at that place was not taken until 1961; from the end of September 1962 the depot, already handling diesels for maintenance, was closed to steam and a beginning made in razing the buildings. The steam allocation of Castle and Hall 4-6-0s, Class 9F 2-10-0s and 0-6-0PT locomotives was transferred mainly to Cardiff East Dock shed, though since 1958 that had been a complete diesel shunter depot, and now had to revert temporarily to steam facilities, the diesel shunters being sent to Cardiff Cathays dmu depot.

Already there were dmu facilities in the carriage plant adjoining Canton, and it was here that some of the Hymeks were serviced and given light maintenance in 1962. Extra servicing facilities were then put in for diesel locomotives, and continued in use for the local shunters and for the Hymeks working the London trains until the servicing shed and fuel facilities at the new depot were ready in October 1963. This part was opened well in advance of the remainder because one of the steam buildings was largely retained and adapted. No diesel locomotives could be allocated for regular heavy maintenance until early 1964, and that was before the official full opening on 18 September 1964. General maintenance allocation approximated to 150 type 3 and type 4 diesel-electrics, 24 Hymeks, around 60 of the standard 350bhp shunters, and a dozen or so of the type 1 Class 9500 0-6-0 diesel-hydraulics.

For heavy maintenance, however, Canton looked after all the diesel-electrics on permanent allocation to the WR, and when the depot was formally opened numbered 317 exclusive of shunters. Canton also was given the heavy maintenance of 43 Hymeks, 62 standard 350bhp shunters, and 96 dmu sets. These figures were well in advance of original proposals, which were to cover only the heavy maintenance of 188 type 3 and type 4 locomotives plus 85 shunters. As Canton did heavy maintenance on both diesel-hydraulics and diesel-electrics the equipment and training were more comprehensive than at Laira, which handled only diesel-hydraulics.

The Canton buildings themselves had the standardised ground-level floor in the servicing side and the three-tier layout in the maintenance building. Distinct from Landore and the second stratum of depots, Canton had some of the stores and offices on an upper level. Only one road of the four ran right through the maintenance shops. It had a 10-ton overhead crane with a 3-ton auxiliary hoist, but a more important part of its equipment was eight synchronised 25-ton hydraulic jacks arranged in two double pairs. They were used to lift heavy diesel-electrics off their bogies for the latter to be run out, for Canton changed six-wheel and eight-wheel diesel-electric bogies as well as the lighter four-wheel type of the allocated diesel-hydraulics. An electrically-operated 40-ton hoist spanning one of the through tracks outside the building was used for lifting one end of a locomotive to release the bogie, and for wagon loading and unloading of those trucks going to or coming from main works. The inside crane was of more than ample capacity to lift Maybach and MAN engines or Voith and Mekydro transmissions, but did not have to cope with the much heavier engines of the diesel-electrics.

The maintenance building was 360ft long by 92ft wide. On three of the stub tracks six diesel-electric shunters could be accommodated; the other three stubs plus the one through track could hold up to 10 type 3 and type 4 locomotives. Tracks themselves were on reinforced concrete walls at a height of 33in above the depressed floor level, and between the rails were pits 54in deep. Thus with the high concrete platforms flanking each berth comfortable three-level access to the locomotives was obtained. Special coupling units at a few points led up to roof discharges to take away oil fumes and steam from train heating boilers under test.

Three roads ran through the servicing shed, and additional stabling tracks were available outside to the east. Three type 4 locomotives could be housed under cover on each shed track, and the planned servicing load was up to 100 large locomotives in 24hr. A jet type washing machine spanned the main western approach track, and below an adjacent track was a pit and a hot water jet installation for washing bogies and underframes in position. The overground six-section main fuel storage had a capacity of 167,000gal, equivalent in 1964 to about three week's consumption, and almost 80 per cent above the capacity first proposed in 1961-62.

The underfloor tyre-reprofiling machine was in the dmu building, away in the carriage maintenance portion of the site, and there the locomotives had to go for skimming up. Original plans had sited this machine on the through track in the locomotive maintenance section, but this would have created a bottle neck. This machine

was of German Hegenscheidt make; that at Laira was the American-designed Atlas-Standard. The essential difference between the two was that the American machine held the axle between centres whereas the German did not. With diesel-hydraulics on these machines the connected wheels in a bogie, other than the pair being skimmed, had to be lifted clear of the rails by hydraulic jacks to allow them to rotate. The machines were expected to true tread and flange, and to ensure that tread diameter of all connected wheels was within 0.01in.

Construction of the London (Old Oak Com-

mon) depot did not begin until 1964, and its formal full opening was on 20 October 1965, though the diesel servicing shed was operating from January that year. Conversion and equipment cost exceeded £500,000. The depot was on part of the site of the large steam shed, and while demolition and reconstruction were going on the depot had to provide decreasing steam facilities and increased dispositions for diesels. The old steam repair shop was adapted to diesel maintenance, and by one of the pits were put the synchronised jacks capable together of lifting over 100 tons.

Because of the site peculiarities the standard side-by-side location of maintenance and servicing buildings could not be adopted; the two were separated by a stores and office block, and were set at an angle to one another. To aid through-flow and reverse arrangements on the servicing side one existing turntable was retained. Only via this could any easy transfer be made between maintenance and servicing sides. Interior arrangements were much as in the other five main diesel depots, but the maintenance section was given seven tracks, perpetuating the old layout with minimum alteration. Two of these tracks normally were reserved for standard shunters. Old Oak Common did major maintenance on the type 2 diesel-hydraulics working in the London area. The 175,000gal fuel tank already existed, having been erected just after World War II when the oil fuel for steam campaign was on.

Conversion and re-equipment of Swindon

Below: *Flow production of D800s in Swindon shops, 1959*

British Railways

Above: *Upturned honeycomb lower portion of D800-type frame, showing main longitudinal 6½in tubes, the two bogie bearers, and dragboxes*
British Railways

works to cope with the change-over was a more comprehensive business spread over some years, for conversion work had to be done on an increasing scale while steam locomotive repairs decreased. This double working, and the need to build new diesel locomotives and give heavy repairs to others before new construction was complete, had certain advantages in that plenty of space was available for extensions and no cut and dried plan on an unknown subject had to be drawn up and followed rigidly.

Operations quite different from any known at Swindon before were needed. Near elimination of forging and smithy work, less plate and boiler work, and reduced foundry and machine shop loading were to be expected even in the first stage, and though the substitute work could be described as mechanical engineering a new light electrical establishment had to be created to deal with the extensive control, safety and auxiliary systems. Moreover, Swindon's introduction to the new was scarcely gradual, for long before completion of the three new locomotives at first ordered the total had been increased to 33, to be built almost on flow-line principles with quite new techniques. Works staff from No 1 downwards through every grade coped with these problems in outstanding fashion except, perhaps, in relation to overall cost.

Great increase in welding and fabrication, and incorporation into interchangeable sub-assemblies of what were thinner plates and sections than were ever found in steam locomotive and tender building were new features. The degree of accuracy in assembly into a 58ft by 8ft 9in by 11ft 6in framework could be achieved only by extensive use of jigs and a carefully worked out sequence. The general design of the D800 superstructure is described in chapter 8, but the method of construction needs a word.

Though 33 locomotives were on order, and more could be foreseen, no process planning was done at Swindon through 1956–62. Sequence planning sheets were provided by the progress and planning office, but they indicated only the items to be made, the shops in which the work was to be done, and the dates by which rough material and finished parts were required. The shop foremen concerned decided how the various parts would be produced, arranged what fixtures they needed, and settled prices with the operators. All this was helped by maintaining close contact with the progress and planning department and by establishment of a small drawing office for jigs and tools.

The D800 frame was begun by welding up several honeycomb sub-assemblies and threading them along the two 6½in diameter tubes as described in chapter 8. First the large centre honeycomb section was welded to the tubes and the wrapped-round floor plate of the section welded on. Working outwards from this section at each end, the intermediate, over-bogie, and end honeycomb sections were welded in sequence to the tubes and the floor skin extended as the frame grew. The completed frame was levelled by twisting and heating, marked off, and cambered ⅝in by pulling down the ends about 2in and applying heat. Then the large floor apertures were cut, the bogie rubbing faces accurately fixed, and the cab inner bulkheads and side frame members welded in position. The roof framing, in two sections, was applied next, followed by the cab top nose framework and then the bottom nose framework. Many of the plates of the honeycomb were machined on the edges to keep the assemblies square and flat, and to control contraction on welding, for unless gaps were uniform the weld would pull more in one place than another.

Before erection on to the whole frame, the outer side skin was pieced together by welding until each side from cab door to cab door was in one piece, and had straps welded to the ends so that the skin could be given some pulling up on the body frame-sections before welding. After this was complete the side apertures for cooling block, windows, etc, were cut out. At this stage the side wall was still rather slack and flabby, and was tensioned by thousands of spot heatings about 1in apart, done by a small welding torch. The end nose skins were added, but in view of the curved shape little tensioning could be applied or flat areas would appear. Finally the insulation pads were put up and the inner perforated light alloy skin fixed to hold them in position.

Many jigs were used, and were made in the shops, simply and without frills; many were on trunnions so that the fixture could be turned over and every possible weld made in the fixture. Some fixtures for bodyside and roof framing were of light construction reinforced with tubes so that the whole could be swung by hand between end pivots when turning upside down, for access from top and bottom was essential for easy welding. Woodworkers' clamps were found best for holding light sections, and hundreds were employed.

Only electric welding was used and there was no spot welding. About 2000 man-hr were spent on a D800 in welding superstructure and attach-

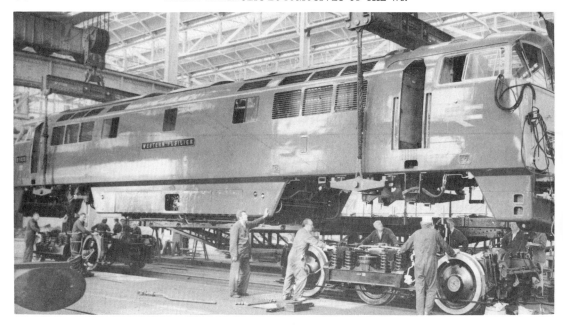

ments. Over a score of AC Murex welding sets were acquired, and had the wide current range of 15 to 330A to suit the wide variety of sheet and plate thicknesses. Few welds in the superstructure were examined by X-ray and fabrications were not relieved of stress. One problem associated with the numerous thin sheets was storage, for it had to be under cover in a dry atmosphere. The steel sheets came to the works pickled and oiled, and the oil had to be removed by sawdust before being worked.

An Eckold machine was used to form the nose ends. It could shrink or stretch the plates, and was used also for angle bending and similar jobs. A Pullmax Major machine cut out curved shapes in plates up to $\frac{3}{8}$in thick, and its high speed nibbler could cut apertures of any shape in the centre of a sheet or cutting in from the edge. An 8ft press brake produced many of the light folded sections used in the framework after first attempts with a hydraulic press; some curved box sections were bent hot on a hand bender.

Most of the superstructure sub-assemblies were produced in one of the old smiths' shops of steam days. Large surface tables about 7in above floor level were used when fabricating the honeycomb frame; they were made up of cast iron blocks about 10ft long and 4ft wide, placed end to end on level runners to get the equivalent of a 60ft by 10ft table. Adjustable height staging was used in the assembly so that the whole superstructure could be encircled and every part reached; in the later stages of locomotive erec-

tion when all equipment could be put in and secured there could be too many men for comfort on the job at once, and custom was to take out again the two diesel engines after they had been lined up and pipe connections adjusted, to give more room. They were re-installed finally only near the end.

Bogie frame welding required a different technique, for the plates were thicker and many of the pads, brackets, and gussets welded in needed machining and squareness to close tolerances. With the D1000-class six-wheel bogies this work grew in complication and in the care needed. Much more use was made of X-rays for weld inspection, and a special building lined with barium bricks and fitted with interlocked doors had to be erected for this work. Bogie side frames were assembled and tack welded on a jig, they were then fully welded up in two stages on manipulators which could provide 360° of rotary movement and 50° of tilt. Only after all brackets and pads were on did the frame go for marking off and machining. For the latter a number of combined shaper-driller-miller machines were employed to do several operations at one setting and help to observe exact centre distances.

In one sense repair and maintenance procedure could be built up and handled more easily by the comparatively low weight and small size of the major components; in another sense it followed major depot procedure in that complete locomotives coming in for repair could be dealt with on the sub-assembly change method. After that was done the components taken out had to be repaired, and this brought workers face to face with tolerance standards and materials quite unknown in steam locomotive practice, and also with components such as pressure-chargers that had in them nothing of reciprocating engine technique. More stripping-shop erecting-shop space was needed for the general repair of a type 4 diesel locomotive than for a main line steam locomotive, but no more total area taking the works as a whole.

Repair organisations and equipment had to be evolved gradually to deal with diesel engines and such appurtenances as fuel pumps, governors and turbo-chargers; hydraulic transmission components; cardan shafts and axle drives; brake equipment including compressors and exhausters; and electrical equipment. A sub-department had to deal with train heating boilers and their controls. Step by step a high standard of work was attained, but much of it was nullified by the lack of organisation and authority in higher echelons of BRB which ruined the spares position and was unable at any time over the years to ensure that troubles were diagnosed and rectified in good time at the depots.

A necessary part of Swindon's new equipment was engine and transmission test beds, for a practical defect of diesel-hydaulics compared with diesel-electrics was that repaired engines of the latter could be tested up to full power when attached to their main generators, and the current fed to resistances while the locomotive remained stationary. Such a method was not possible with hydraulic drive, and special test cubicles with dynamometers had to be put in at a cost exceeding £500,000. Not until 1965 was the equipment ready to deal with engines of 1100 to 1740bhp, and give them running-in and calibration tests. The complete testing station had a water cooling plant with hot and cold underground sumps, cooling towers and pumps, rooms for calibrating and checking instruments, and testing lubricating oils.

Special test rigs also were evolved for transmission blocks, axle drives and other details, for it was an axiom that any part of an engine or transmission which went out on a repaired locomotive, or as a spare sub-assembly to a depot, should have been proved to function properly and to have been calibrated and set, so that a depot had nothing to do but put in the replacement part without further check unless a specific instruction for a running-in period on secondary services was received with the part.

Above: *Gearbox of Maybach Mekydro K104 transmission under repair at Swindon. Note small size of four-stage gears to transmit over 1000hp; control block to rhs of gears; converter removed*
British Railways

Left: *Wheeling the last WR diesel-hydraulic locomotive to be given a general repair at Swindon*
British Railways

Below: *NBL/MAN type L12V/21B engine overhaul at Swindon*
British Railways

CHAPTER 13

LOCOMOTIVE AND EQUIPMENT PERFORMANCE

THROUGHOUT the 1960s all large diesel locomotives on BR had their troubles and brought their disillusionments. They have them still, and through 1973–74 the leading types of diesel-electrics rarely showed availabilities above 70 per cent on the BR definition of that term. Through the first half of the 1960s, and even later, there was never strong central direction capable of correct evaluation on competent and unbiased grounds, or of authority and ability to build up and insist on rapid and correct diagnosis of defects, and equally rapid and effective correction. This was the same on diesel-electrics and diesel-hydraulics, and was responsible for a large part of the chronically poor performance of nearly every BR type.

Effects of this lack of central direction were aggravated by the policy, initiated with the new BRB of 1963, of cutting down stocks of spares, and of ordering them on methods associated more with tinned foods, with the important difference that tinned-food types of ordering and distribution could not be achieved with diesel locomotive parts. At Swindon diesel-hydraulics requiring two or three days' work were held idle for more than the same number of weeks awaiting small spares, and the tightening up of supplies was such that at one time there was not a single spare cylinder liner of any type in stock.

This policy showed up well in the books of the finance and stores departments, but was hardly an aid to good availability and utilisation. It upset the economics of diesel traction as a whole, and deranged the carefully worked out maintenance and repair procedure. WR main depots had to cannibalise engines and transmissions to keep some of their locomotives going, while Swindon meanwhile had an accumulation of locomotives awaiting spares. Much of the reduced availability of Western and Hymek classes in the second half of 1964 and through 1965 was due directly to this cause.

WR diesel-hydraulic locomotive performance has to be viewed against these backgrounds in both absolute and comparative senses. Few major troubles arose straight from engines or hydraulic portions of the transmissions. Many of the faults came from the factors noted above; others from accepted unsuitability of parts for their functions without much effort to get them rectified; more from almost trifling accessories; and others from unsatisfactory design.

Of the last-named the most important on the WR were those associated with the K-M bogies and final drives in the D800s and D1000s. This bogie had given satisfactory service up to 75mph in Germany, but from 80mph upwards was unsuitable, and even possibly dangerous. Insufficient lateral motion of the bogie relative to the body, and a high resistance to what there was,

Left: *Input end of L630rV transmission; two mounting faces on the end and two on the side*

Right: *Four-wheel K-M bogie as applied to D800 locomotives. Body weight was taken via pins in the hole in the buckle of the inverted laminated springs*

British Railways

resulted in what was nearly a rigid lateral connection between the two parts. Rotary movement of the bogie relative to the body was free and easy; but main lateral flexibility was solely in the rubber bushes of the bell-crank and link pivoting mechanism, and it produced a resistance to side movement of about 100 tons/in. The only other flexibility in a transverse direction was the small amount in the rubber bushes of the axlebox arms and side suspension links; but the sum of all this was an equivalent swing link length of but $1\frac{1}{4}$in and a resistance to lateral movement of 25 tons/in. This accounted for the high frequency of nearly $2\frac{1}{2}$ oscillations per second above 80mph, set up when the flanges struck points and crossings, and when the locomotive ran over poor rail joints or other small faults of alignment. Then the bogie was suddenly displaced sideways and more or less wrenched the body over with it. Once the tyres began to wear, oscillation was prolonged; when the 80mph limit was imposed a restriction to 50,000 miles between tyre reprofiling also was established.

Long tests began in the summer of 1959. Eventually the whole bell-crank and link pivoting gear was removed; the body was then suspended and its lateral motion controlled by the side suspension links, which acted also as swing links with their true length of 15in. Twin lateral hydraulic dampers were inserted in each bogie to absorb any residual lateral oscillation, and twin rubber side stops, with $\frac{3}{4}$in gap, were put in to ensure the stability of the side bearing springs. Body and bogie then were located longitudinally by the curved traction and braking thrust faces, which had to be altered slightly to cope with the relative side movement.

In 1960 trials of the revised bogie began on D813, and numerous runs made with measuring equipment at all speeds and different degrees of tyre wear. All requirements were met, and without the need to give the tyre a different profile as suggested by K-M. When both mechanical and civil engineers were satisfied and the speed ceiling had reverted to 90mph in 1963, the practical position had become complicated by the completion of many D1000s, which had the same bogie principle in six-wheel form. By the time the revised bogie was fully accepted for 90mph the modifications could be applied new only to the last five D1000s to come from Crewe, that is, to the five transferred there from Swindon. Priority through 1963 was given to the alteration of D1000 bogies, for the operating department needed the 90mph version for accelerations programmed for the 1963 winter timetables; after experience with the first few conversions the large rubber side blocks between superstructure and bogies in the D1000s were replaced by metal. The D800s were converted gradually through 1963–64.

Before D1000-class bogies began to cause serious concern, D1000 itself was in trouble after a month or so in traffic, with seizure of roller bearings on the transmission output shaft; both transmission blocks of D1001, then just going into traffic, were removed for a check inspection. This trouble continued for a long period, and at a later stage the whole D1000 fleet was withdrawn briefly, but normal working was restored after a few days when not more than 20 per cent of the locomotives were seen to be affected. The

Above: *Maybach MD650 engine of 1100bhp ready for testing after strip-down and repair*
British Railways

Below: *First of the second Swindon production, D803* Albion, *passes Dawlish with the up Mayflower in August 1959*
Derek Cross

cause was not so quickly determined, and was not fully diagnosed and cured until 1964.

The horizontal torque reaction members on the axle drive castings led to rapid angular acceleration of the cardans whenever axles and boxes rose or fell relative to the bogie frame; this wore the splines in the cardans, and relative movement and stresses went back into the intermediate gearbox, and beyond as far as the hydraulic transmission output. At low speeds and high tractive efforts the torque reaction could be transmitted wholly to the cardans instead of being taken up and cushioned by the torque arm bearings, and this accentuated the troubles.

Again the solution was simple, but the investigations preceding it were lengthy, complicated and expensive, and went into the normal and parasitic forces through the whole drive system to all three axles. The horizontal torque arms had to be changed to the vertical type, and quite different proportions and deflection coefficients introduced into the cushioning. Fortunately this could be done without much modification to the bogie; but the work to be done reduced the locomotive availability. This trouble, again, was peculiar to BR. The original torque reaction design was applied elsewhere to diesel-hydraulics of 1800 to 4000hp, and continues to run without complaint 10 to 12 years after application.

One further disorder that affected D1000

availability was the dynastarter cardan drive taken by gears from the primary shaft of the Voith transmission, and in which criticals occurred around 250rpm whenever the engine was started or was being shut down. This loosened the auxiliary drive gear wheels within the transmission block. Eventually a much softer flexible coupling in the drive line brought a cure. This could hardly be called a major defect but with other work being undertaken at the time full attention was not given to this particular aspect though it led to many failures in service, and 2½ years elapsed between the first defects and the general adoption of the remedy.

These were the principal disorders of the D1000s, but by no means the only ones. Many reported failures, and much of the low availability, were due to inattention at depots to small parts, neglect of which led subsequently to much more substantial damage elsewhere. The Westerns were not alone in this, but added to the work of altering the bogies and the torque reaction system, and making about 60 small design modifications, it resulted in the class being rostered during the summer and autumn of 1964 on an availability of only 60 per cent, this descending to the level over two years or so of the D1 diesel-electrics.

Hymeks also had their moments despite getting off to a generally good start. Difficulties began when little more than half the locomotives were in service, and led to deferred delivery of some of the remainder in the hope that the trouble could be rectified quickly. Early in 1963 defects in the control block of the Mekydro transmission brought malfunctioning of the gear shifts and in some cases this led to other consequential damage. The cause arose from unwarranted changes in manufacturing tolerances, introduced when the K184 began to go from individual production into series production at Friedrichshafen; strengthening of one or two parts also was indicated. Over nearly a year while these matters were under investigation and rectification, the MD870 engines in many Hymeks were derated to 1350bhp and the first gear step of the four in the transmission was locked out. When the tolerances were put right and the hubs of two gear wheels strengthened the engines were reset to 1740 bhp.

Second major trouble was in the main cardan shaft between engine and transmission, and in the auxiliary cardan shaft drive to the dynastarter, the two troubles being associated. A reduction in the stiffness of the flexible coupling did not improve matters, and a mathematical study of the whole shaft system in relation to criticals and vibration torques was begun. The cure was an additional flexible coupling at the transmission end of the short primary main shaft, and a softer coupling at the engine end, which tuned the whole system and eliminated excessive wear on the splines of the cardan shaft that had forced attention to the whole primary shaft system. This, and a softer coupling in the auxiliary drive, also eased the troubles with the dynastarter.

With only two engine makes and two transmission makes the performances in these fields can be reviewed against those backgrounds rather than on the basis of locomotive classes. The 66 NBL/MAN engines in D833–65 and the 52 in D6306–57 never seemed to attain their potentialities. Incessant small troubles developed in many directions, but from the beginning major problems were encountered with constant defects in exhaust systems and split manifold branches which often overloaded repair facilities at depots. At that time (1960–62) some depots were incomplete and full staffs untrained, and many replacements had to be fabricated at Swindon. Part of the trouble was that NBL-built engines had exhaust manifolds and branches of mild steel. Augsburg-built engines of the same model in the Blue Pullman units had Ni-resist steel and the troubles were largely obviated. Serious exhaust leakage also upset pressure-charger working by starvation, and the effects continued into the engine.

Locking plates on big ends were defective, and big-end bolt failures sometimes led to more internal damage. Softer couplings had to be inserted between engine and transmission. Piston and combustion troubles were not unknown, possibly because of the high rating for a conventional engine which was unconventional in having no piston cooling, not even the squirt from a pipe in the rod for gudgeon pin lubrication. Though the fire ring was chrome-plated great wear developed in the ring groove, so that sealing became imperfect.

From the mid-1960s the very simplicity of the design suggested that determined efforts should be made to rectify some of the recurrent defects. This approach was supported by the fact that one L12V18/21B engine had passed the BS 100-hr type test in 1960, though the 1957 test to UIC rules of the L12V18/21A model had been only at 800bhp and 1400rpm. Therefore one engine was sent to the British Internal Combustion Engine Research Association (BICERA) for

Above: *Set of cylinder liners from a Maybach MD650 engine after 495,000 miles; numbers on barrels correspond to cylinder numbers*
Motoren und Turbinen Union

Below: *Crankpin and disc webs of a Maybach MD650 engine after 470,000 miles. The main roller bearings fit in the recess in the web circumference*
Motoren und Turbinen Union

lengthy tests and any necessary modifications, but to no purpose. Not many drivers would put D833–65 into the seventh power notch for any length of time. All MAN-engined D800s were withdrawn between 1969 and 1971.

Much greater in number, the Maybach engines attracted more attention; at one time the number and type of reported defects were so large and unusual in relation to installations of similar engines in other countries, that a detailed study was made of every reported defect over a 24-week period through the winter of 1965–66 and covering almost $6\frac{1}{2}$ million miles. The casualties recorded are analysed in Table XV. The BR definition of a casualty or failure was defined as one that produced a lateness of 5min or more on passenger trains and 10min or more on goods trains.

These investigations showed that many defects put down on WR sheets through this 24 weeks and over previous years to main constituents such as engines and transmissions were basically nothing of the sort, and were defects of auxiliaries and accessories which, because they were not remedied when reported, eventually produced consequential damage in large components. Many

Table XV—Analysis of Casualties; Maybach-Engined Locomotives

Loco Class & Nos	D7000-7100		D800-29, D831-32, D866-70		D1000-73	
Maybach Engine Model	1 x MD870		2 x MD650		2 x MD655	
	Casualties in 24 weeks and 6.35 million miles					
	number	per cent	number	per cent	number	per cent
Diesel engine	6	7.5	2	2.5	16	6.4
Cooling equipment[1]	24	30.0	27	34.2	89	35.3
Hydraulic transmission	7	8.75	3	3.8	21	8.6
Cardan shafts	2	2.5	2	2.5	2	0.8
Final drives	2	2.5	—	—	3	1.2
Drive of auxiliary equipment	4	5.0	—	—	3	1.2
Electrical & control apparatus	16	20.0	28	35.6	54	21.9
Brake equipment	8	10.0	8	10.0	22	8.8
Train-heating boiler & controls	2	2.5	4	5.0	18	7.2
Miscellaneous mechanical portion	9	11.25	5	6.4	21	8.6
TOTAL	80	100	79	100	249	100

[1] Including thermostatic control

cooler-group defects were booked as engine failures because of later breakdowns there.

Maybach reputation for cracked cylinder heads became notorious. In 1965 there were 326, that is $7\frac{1}{2}$ per cent of the total in service. The BRB cme wrote of them in 1966: 'In view of the large number of cracked cylinder heads which are clearly thermally overloaded . . .' but did not go on to say that the thermal overloading was caused principally by cooler-group defects that had received no attention. Yet close investigation showed that over 60 per cent of cracked heads reported through 1965 and the first few months of 1966 were due to water shortage and other unrectified cooler group defects.

These shortcomings were mainly poor fan control, improperly working shutters, unreliable safety devices, poor quality hoses and pipe connections with resultant water and high pressure oil leakage, indifferent supports for high pressure hydrostatic pumps and pipes, poor pipe venting, and leakage from header tanks. Temperature control devices were quite unreliable, and settings were actually affected in an incorrect way by ambient temperature and pressure. No provision was made for accurate calibration and sealing; in some cases actual setting lay between 110° and 135°C contrasting with the specified 91/92°C. No wonder cylinder heads failed. From the same cause came a quota of MAN engine troubles.

Following a mistake in terminology when ordering a British lubricating oil corresponding to the accepted German quality, an unsuitable oil was selected at first and brought troubles in valves and main roller bearing housings. The problem was cleared up and the correct oil later specified, but six months elapsed before it was ordered. Meanwhile engines were allowed to run under deteriorating conditions. In 1963 the Crane seal for water pumps was recommended by BSE as being more suitable than the seal fitted. Though the Crane was already standard on certain other BR diesels it was not fitted to WR diesel-hydraulics before 1966, though in 1965 Bristol Bath Road depot alone changed 36 charge-air water pumps and 35 engine water pumps because of leakage on MD655 and MD870 engines.

A not uncommon sight for some years was serious water leakage down the sides of the D1000s. This arose because holes were cut in the header tank in the roof to check whether interiors were being affected adversely by treatment of the cooling water. After the check these holes were simply covered by thin plate and 'secured' by self-threading screws rather than by equally simple water-tight welding. One result was that three to five gallons of cooling water could be lost on the way up from Exeter to London. Elimination of losses by evaporation from the cooling water circuit was recommended by BSE in April 1964 by the fitting of small valves; this was not done inside two years.

Difference in quality between licensee-made parts and those from the parent works is not an unusual feature arising from licence agreements. Here it was shown in definitive fashion, and MD655 and MD870 licence-built engines were shown to be $2\frac{1}{2}$ to 4 times more prone to trouble than the MD650s built by the parent company. The forked big ends with wide spread and low unit bearing loads had given so little trouble in about 800 MD engines spread throughout the world that they had almost been forgotten as a vital engine component. BSE-made big-end bearings soon began to heat, and in the 24-week investigation period 28 rods in MD655 (D1000 class) and MD870 (Hymek) engines had failures of one kind or another. At this period the two original MD650 engines put into D800 had given 21,000hr of service each without any rod defect at all. To test this comparison one BSE-made MD655 was given Maybach-made rods and big-end bearings, and another was given BSE improved rods and bearings. The former showed no defects after more than 3000hr of service; the latter was dismantled after 3270hr and the rods and bearings were considered unfit for further service in the observed condition.

Cracks in welded crankcases also were found in licence-built engines, though no crack had been reported in 338 similar crankcases in MD655 and MD870 engines in other countries. A good proportion of turbo-charger failures was due to an inexpensive roller bearing adopted by the licensee, and, on their recommendation, by Swindon in making repairs. Because of replacements of such parts, and other work done at the time of the replacements, comparatively few licence-built engines went the full expected

period between major overhauls, though three of the early Friedrichshafen MD650s did not get a routine major strip-down and overhaul until 25,670, 26,150 and 29,650hr respectively, equal to distances of 850,000 to 870,000 miles.

Transmissions gave rise neither to so much trouble nor to so much comment as long as the safety devices operated. In one or two instances where they did not, gear wheels reached blue heat. Of the first 20 million Mekydro-K104 miles the failure rate was one in 378,000 miles related to everything within the transmission block; 10 sets ran 345,000 to 380,000 miles each without being taken out of the locomotive for any reason whatever, and another seven covered above 280,000 miles without disturbance. These mileages corresponded to the range of 10,000 to 15,000hr of service, but the grinding marks on most of the change-speed wheels were still visible. WR practice refrained from removing transmissions from locomotives for periodic overhaul, as early test inspections had shown internal condition to be good enough for the main block to be left intact until some incipient defect came to notice, or until the service hours had risen to a very high figure.

For the routine opening up, inspection and main repair of 85 model K104 and 108 K184 transmissions (including spares) one inspector and six or seven men were enough at Swindon through most of the 1960s, and the number of units under repair at a time after the Hymek control blocks were rectified was three or four, rising to six or seven when a larger number of locomotives than usual came to their overhaul periods at the same time. The Voith units had a similar standard of performance.

An astonishing number of failures occurred in train heating boilers and their controls, and to brakes and other miscellaneous mechanical portion items—equipment with which over 70 years of experience had been gained, and which had nothing to do with engines or transmissions or controls. This was especially so with the D1000s. Train heating boilers, or rather their controls, were a recurrent seasonal defect, and availability curves regularly dropped during very cold weather.

Left: *Pair of wheels and claw clutches from a Mekydro K104 drive after 15,500 service hours in a D800; grinding marks still visible*
Motoren und Turbinen Union

The large number of defects in control and minor electric circuits and apparatus was common to all BR diesels. In 1961 one BR Officer, R. C. S. Low, stated in a paper *British Railway Experience With Diesel Traction* that 50 to 70 per cent of the failures reported from the whole stock of line service locomotives were due to cooling equipment and electrical and control apparatus. Many stoppages of diesel locomotives of over £100,000 capital cost were due to undeveloped items costing £20 or less. Another author, E. Bennett, of English Electric, stated in 1965 (Inst of Loco Engineers) that 40 per cent of all recorded failures in EE diesels on BR were in bought-out components.

During the period of the investigations noted above the availability of the Hymeks (by then cured of their control block and cardan shaft troubles) was steady between 75 and 78 per cent; the 37 Maybach-engined D800s showed availability fluctuating between 69 and 79 per cent. The D1000s were in one of their bad periods when availability varied between 54 and 60 per cent only, but over 25 per cent of all their reported casualties were due to mechanical portion details, and another 35 per cent to those defects in cooling systems already outlined. The small proportion of boiler casualties in the Hymeks resulted from many of the class being on freight duties where the boiler was not in use.

The inability of BTC and BRB headquarters to get depots staffed and run so that faults could be diagnosed quickly and rectified at once, with co-ordination between headquarters, depots and works to deal adequately with recurrent faults, led to availability of all BR type 2, 3 and 4 diesels remaining below figures expected when the modernisation plan was initiated. Typical averages for WR diesel-hydraulics over a year in the mid 1960s are shown in Fig 20. The high level of availability given by the D6300s was not always like this, but the locomotives of that class were diagrammed so leniently that on the BR definition of availability good results were attained fairly easily.

Though low according to expectations, availabilities shown in Fig 20 are much better than those of steam locomotives. During the full period of steam traction on BR many steam classes of high reputation had availabilities below 60 per cent, and even well-cared-for top class power on high diagrammed mileages rarely went above the mid 60s, even on a basis of 313 working days a year.

Despite largely disappointing availabilities WR diesel-hydraulics, particularly D800s and Hymeks, made good mileages in their respective power classes. Over the first nine or ten years of life D800–32 averaged over 90,000 miles a year, and the prototype D800 reached one million miles

Fig 20 *Availability curves of Western Region diesel locomotives over one year in the mid-1960s*

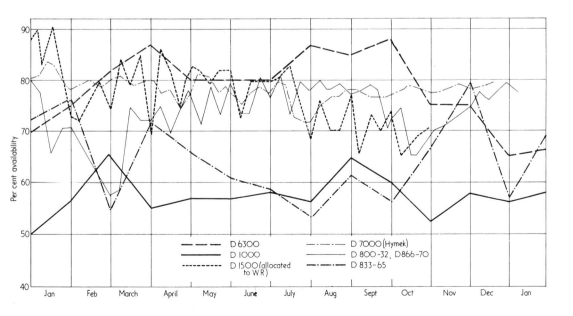

in just over 10 years. D833–65 showed individual annual mileages 10 to 11 per cent less. Of the steam engines they replaced the King-class 4–6–0s did not average above 55,000 miles annually in BR days or the Castles above 50,000 miles. This meant 60 to 80 per cent improvement by the diesel-hydraulics.

Figures officially displayed by BR at the CIMAC London conference in April 1965 showed on analysis that D800–32 and D866–70 had averaged 95,100 miles a year since being put into service; D833–65 had averaged 80,000, and D1000- 73 showed 65,400 miles. Type 3 Hymeks, naturally not much rostered on high mileage diagrams, averaged 60,000 miles a year. Of the principal diesel-electrics the then largely new D1500s had made 69,300 miles a year and the D1 class 56,750 miles.

Subsequent official attempts to explain this away showed that the two diesel-electric types worked a much higher proportion of their total time on freight trains, but in 1963 the chief technical adviser to the BRB had shown such locomotives on 1300-ton freights to have a load factor of only 24 per cent spread over the running time. Another leading BR official recorded in 1965 that one of those diesel-electrics in heavy freight work needed 70 to 100 per cent of its rated power for only six per cent of its total time under power. Despite the many maledictions and disappointing availabilities, the Maybach-engined D800s were giving far greater mileages at higher load factors than the diesel-electrics, and the D1000s were nearly equal to the D1500s, and despite shocking availabilities were making 16 per cent greater mileage at higher load factor than the D1 engines with equally low availability. As to the Hymeks, their annual individual mileage from new was 15 per cent better than that of any type 3 diesel-electric.

The BR cme stated in the *Railway Gazette* of 17 September 1965 that casualties over an unstated and undefined period were 33 per cent more in the diesel-hydraulics than in diesel-electrics within type 4 power class. Yet as the WR diesel-hydraulics of D800 type made 30 per cent greater mileage on a higher load factor than the D1500s the only inference can be that the diesel-hydraulic reported casualties were of a minor nature, whereas those of the diesel-electrics were of a major character. Moreover, the major defects of the diesel-electrics were not reported casualties; they were the engine-frame cracks and numerous other troubles that led to over 700 engines being sent back to the maker's works at the rate of one a day to be repaired, rebuilt and rebalanced, with a decidedly adverse effect on BR diesel locomotive traction as a whole.

CHAPTER 14

RUNDOWN AND CONCLUSION

A HIGH level decision in 1967 to reduce substantially both the number and number of classes of BR diesel locomotives led to the planned withdrawal of all diesel-hydraulics by the end of 1974, and for their replacement on the WR by standard diesel-electrics which had become surplus on other regions by reduction in traffic, improved diagramming and by the spread of LMR electrification. Nothing can be said against such a policy. Diminution of types was most desirable, and though none of the diesel-electrics was any better in performance than the diesel-hydraulics, the latter, in 1967, formed little more than 10 per cent of the line service diesel stock. Moreover not only the transmissions but also the general types of engine installed were quite different from those in the other 90 per cent. Elimination of the diesel-hydraulics would also permit termination of all repair and heavy maintenance work at Swindon, for the other establishments of British Rail Engineering, the workshops organisation, were already capable of handling all diesel-electrics.

The D600s were withdrawn at the end of 1967. Of the D6300 class 29 were withdrawn by the end of 1969; then there was a reprieve, and no WR diesel-hydraulic of any type was taken out of stock during 1970. Withdrawals of D6300s were resumed in 1971 and the two last of the type were taken out officially on 1 January 1972. Many MAN-engined D800s (BR Class 42) were in store for some months in 1969 but only three were officially withdrawn in that year; the remainder lasted until 1971. The Maybach-engined D800s (BR Class 43) were withdrawn in 1971–72, and might have lasted another year if the 1968 efforts to fit continuous air brake equipment had been successful.

All Hymeks were scheduled for withdrawal by the end of 1973; but shortage of motive power on the WR due to the generally low availability of all diesels, and the reluctance of other regions to transfer power at the planned rate, resulted in 10 still being actively at work in February 1974, and with a few of those officially withdrawn still being cannibalised at depots. Those at work were D7001/11/6/7/8/22/6/8/9/93. All Westerns were to go before the end of 1974, but in February of that year 57 were still at work, though

no general repairs were given after September 1973. All 57 were based at Laira.

Should the final D1000 last until the end of 1974, then diesel-hydraulic performance on the WR will have exceeded 3200 locomotive-years, and attained around 4900 engine-years and the same number of hydraulic-transmission years. In the 16 years of diesel-hydraulic traction above 160 million locomotive-miles were accumulated. Were they worthwhile?

Construction cost of diesel-hydraulic locomotives at Swindon was inordinate. Had the same levels been applied to diesel-electrics they, too, would have been economically impracticable. Whatever the saving in fuel or by any other means, it could not recoup the extra book charges for the interest and depreciation. The 38 members of the D800 class built at Swindon averaged £121,430 apiece, more or less the same as the final price of a D1500 Co–Co diesel-electric of 10 per cent greater output, though admittedly over 500 of the latter were constructed against 38. To the benefit of the BTC and to the detriment of NBL, the price paid for the 33 Glasgow-built D800s was some thousands less. These were not the general run of diesel-hydraulic prices, of which the best example is the D6306–57 batch at around £64,000 for 1100bhp from a single engine. Standard single-engine B–Bs of 1000bhp could be obtained in Europe in 1960–63 for less than £60,000, and in the same period B–B 80-ton twin-engine 2700bhp locomotives cost no more than £100,000 apiece on the basis of 20 off.

Worst of the WR diesel-hydraulics, the Westerns, paralleled the D1-class (BR classes 44–46) diesel-electrics in low availability but made 10 per cent greater mileage a year under higher load factor. The Maybach D800s made higher annual individual mileages than any type 4 diesel-electric and the less successful MAN-engined D800s approached the average produced by the English Electric D200s (BR class 40). In each transmission category in type 4 power the worst performers were the classes designed and built by the BR—the D1000 diesel-hydraulics and the D1 diesel-electrics; next lowest was the D1500 class designed largely by BR and built by an outside contractor.

Number of casualties reported in diesel-

Above: *One of the first diesel-hydraulic locomotives,
No D601, on the down Cornish Riviera at Reading
West in 1958, its initial year of service*

M. W. Earley

Below: Western Fusilier *about to leave Swindon
in September 1973 after being given the factory's
last general repair to any diesel-hydraulic locomotive. Extra hose at front for Westinghouse
continuous air brake*

British Railways

hydraulics often were greater, *per capita*, than in diesel-electrics, but apart from the few more troublesome problems detailed in the preceding chapter they were not of great moment and *could* have been rectified easily, even though they were not. That aspect was almost inherent in diesel-hydraulics with quick running engines. Diesel-electrics also had a large percentage of all reported defects due to cooling equipment and other accessories. They also and more seriously had major troubles with the slow-speed engines, which led in one case to 263 locomotives being given new engines of another make, and in type 4 power to more than 700 large engines being returned to the maker in rotation through 1966–67 to deal with fractured engine blocks, need for rebalancing, and attention to numerous recurrent defects such as liner cracking and corrosion. The output had to be reduced from 2750 to 2500bhp.

Availabilities of the two principal BR-designed diesel-electrics, the D1 and D1500 (BR Classes 44–47), were such that normally well over 200 locomotives were out of service daily, and it was not uncommon to see 35 to 38 of them in Crewe works alone. These ineffective locomotives represented around £24 million of invested capital lying idle throughout the year, and this was quite

apart from the time lost back at the maker's works. WR diesel-hydraulics at least never had such a fiasco marked against them.

Real troubles with the diesel-hydraulics were the same as those with the diesel-electrics, inability to diagnose rapidly and correctly reported defects and to take immediate action to rectify them. Nor was there any true co-ordination to deal with recurrent defects. This situation is nearly as bad in 1974 as it was in 1964; the availabilities throughout the years of 70–73 per cent accepted by successions of higher BR authorities would have put diesel traction outside economic consideration in most European countries and others further afield, and would not be tolerated for three months on such railways. This disastrous situation, the cure of which was accorded low priority, not only ruined the performance of diesel-hydraulics and of those diesel-electrics that had some potentialities, but led a commission from a large European national railway that studied BR diesel traction on the spot when some 2000 locomotives were in hand, to state in its report in 1964: 'British Railways are in no way organised for diesel traction.' They could have added 'diesel-hydraulic *or* diesel-electric.'

Table XVI—Leading dimensions of WR diesel-hydraulic locomotives

Class		D600	D6300 (6300-5)	D6300 (6306-57)	D800 (800-2)	D800 (803-29, 31-32, 866-70)	D800 (830)	D800 (833-65)	D7000	D1000
Builder		NBL	NBL	NBL	Swindon	Swindon	Swindon	NBL	B-P	Swindon (30) Crewe (44)
Axle arrangement		A1A-A1A	B-B	B-B	B-B	B-B	B-B	B-B	B-B	C-C
Engine type		MAN	MAN	MAN	Maybach	Maybach	Paxman	MAN	Maybach	Maybach
Total bhp		2000	1000	1100	2070	2270	2270	2200	1740	2760
Transmission type		Voith	Voith	Voith	Mekydro	Mekydro	Mekydro	Voith	Mekydro	Voith
Loco weight, empty	tons	108.7	62.3	60.5	69.0	69.0	68.3	71.4	68.8	98.4
Loco weight, full	tons	117.4	68.0	65.0	78.6	78.6	77.8	80.8	75.4	108.0
Overall length	ft in	65-0	46-8½	46-8½	60-0	60-0	60-0	60-0	51-8¾	68-0
Body width	ft in	8-8	8-8	8-8	8-8⅜	8-8⅜	8-8⅜	8-8⅜	8-10	8-8½
Max height	ft in	12-10	12-10	12-10	12-9½	12-9½	12-9½	12-9½	12-10½	12-11¾
Wheel dia	in	43.0	43.0	43.0	39.5	39.5	39.5	39.5	45.0	43.0
Bogie wheelbase	ft in	15-0	8-6	8-6	10-6	10-6	10-6	10-6	10-6	12-2
Bogie pivot pitch	ft in	35-0	23-0	23-0	37-9	37-9	37-9	37-9	25-6	42-6
Total wheelbase	ft In	50-0	31-6	31-6	48-3	48-3	48-3	48-3	36-0	54-8
Max designed speed	mph	90	75	75	90	90	90	90	90	90
Fuel capacity	gal	800	450	450	800	800	800	800	900	850
Boiler water capacity	gal	1000	500	500	940	940	940	940	800	980
Heating boiler type		Spanner Ia	Spanner Ia	Clayton (20) Vapor (32)	Spanner Ia	Spanner I (15) Spanner III(1) Vapor (19)	Vapor	Vapor	Vapor (45) Spanner III (56)	Spanner III

ACKNOWLEDGEMENTS

The warmest thanks of the author for invaluable help given in the compilation of this book are due to: Keith Montague, Ray Smith, Ken May, Brian Wakefield, T. McKinlay, David Patrick, Ivo Peters, J. W. P. Rowledge, Alex Eversmann, M. von Kienlin, F. Schüttel, Rolf Keller, and W. Paetzold, and A. C. L. Sly.

Author and publisher also are indebted to the many photographers who have provided prints and permission to use them.

Light alloy nameplate of D812
British Railways

INDEX